MAY 2001

Harriet Beecher Stowe's
UNCLE TOM'S CABIN

NOTES

A CONTEMPORARY
LITERARY VIEWS BOOK

Edited and with an Introduction by
HAROLD BLOOM

3 5 7 9 8 6 4 2

Cover Illustration: Schomburg Center for Research in Black Culture, New York Public Library

Library of Congress Cataloging-in-Publication Data

Harriet Beecher Stowe's Uncle Tom's cabin / Harold Bloom, editor.
p. cm – (Bloom's notes)
Includes bibliographical references and index.
Summary: Includes a brief biography of Harriet Beecher Stowe, thematic and structural analysis of the work, critical views, and an index of themes and ideas.
ISBN 0-7910-3672-3
1. Stowe, Harriet Beecher, 1811–1896. Uncle Tom's cabin. 2. Plantation life in literature. 3. Southern States—In literature. 4. Afro-Americans in literature. 5. Slavery in literature. 6. Slaves in literature. [1. Stowe, Harriet Beecher, 1811–1896 Uncle Tom's cabin. 2. American literature—History and criticism.] I. Bloom, Harold. II. Series.
PS2954.U6H37 1996
813'.3—dc20
95-35221
CIP
AC

Chelsea House Publishers
1974 Sproul Road, Suite 400
P.O. Box 914
Broomall, PA 19008-0914

Contents

User's Guide

This volume is designed to present biographical, critical, and bibliographical information on Harriet Beecher Stowe and *Uncle Tom's Cabin*. Following Harold Bloom's introduction, there appears a detailed biography of the author, discussing the major events in her life and her important literary works. Then follows a thematic and structural analysis of the work, in which significant themes, patterns, and motifs are traced. An annotated list of characters supplies brief information on the chief characters in the work.

A selection of critical extracts, derived from previously published material by leading critics, then follows. The extracts consist of statements by the author on her work, early reviews of the work, and later evaluations down to the present day. The items are arranged chronologically by date of first publication. A bibliography of Stowe's writings (including a complete listing of all books she wrote, cowrote, edited, and translated), a list of additional books and articles on her and on *Uncle Tom's Cabin,* and an index of themes and ideas conclude the volume.

Harold Bloom is Sterling Professor of the Humanities at Yale University and Henry W. and Albert A. Berg Professor of English at the New York University Graduate School. He is the author of twenty books and the editor of more than thirty anthologies of literature and literary criticism.

Professor Bloom's works include *Shelley's Mythmaking* (1959), *The Visionary Company* (1961), *Blake's Apocalypse* (1963), *Yeats* (1970), *A Map of Misreading* (1975), *Kabbalah and Criticism* (1975), and *Agon: Towards a Theory of Revisionism* (1982). *The Anxiety of Influence* (1973) sets forth Professor Bloom's provocative theory of the literary relationships between the great writers and their predecessors. His most recent books are *The American Religion* (1992) and *The Western Canon* (1994).

Professor Bloom earned his Ph.D. from Yale University in 1955 and has served on the Yale faculty since then. He is a 1985 MacArthur Foundation Award recipient and served as the Charles Eliot Norton Professor of Poetry at Harvard University in 1987–88. He is currently the editor of the Chelsea House series Major Literary Characters and Modern Critical Views, and other Chelsea House series in literary criticism.

Introduction

HAROLD BLOOM

Uncle Tom's Cabin or, Life among the Lowly was published on March 20, 1852, and by about a year after its publication was reported to have sold over 300,000 copies in the United States and well over another two million throughout the world, both in the original and in translation. As Edmund Wilson noted, it lost almost all its popularity after the Civil War (which it had helped to cause), and did not regain a wide audience until the second half of our century. Wilson speculated that both sides, North and South, did not want to be reminded of the issue of black slavery for nearly a century after Emancipation. And yet, rereading it now, I have to agree with Wilson that it is a permanent and impressive work, forceful and fierce, a book worthy of the spirit of John Brown, who prophetically warned the nation: "Without the shedding of blood, there is no remission of sins." As a narrative, *Uncle Tom's Cabin* has its weaknesses, but the book is powerful in its characterizations. Wilson shrewdly said that the characters "express themselves a good deal better than the author expresses herself." I find this to be particularly true of Aunt Chloe and Uncle Tom, of Eliza and of George Harris and, most of all, of that magnificent and mythological monster, the superbly wicked Simon Legree, a plantation owner yet a New England Yankee, as Wilson reminded us.

Harriet Beecher Stowe, though moved by a biblical sense of urgency, was too shrewd to write her book as a mere polemic against the South. Her concerns, and her anguish, were patriotic but national, and *Uncle Tom's Cabin* indicts both North and South, in the name of Christianity. Because an "Uncle Tom" has become a black and liberal term of contempt, we need to begin reading the book by cleansing ourselves of our period prejudices. Uncle Tom is not only the novel's heroic protagonist but indeed is the only authentic Christian in Stowe's vision of her nation. A literary character greatly admired by Tolstoy and by Dickens deserves our careful regard. For Stowe, Uncle Tom is the Christ-like martyr more truly crucified by the North than by the South, for New England had accepted the Fugitive Slave Act of 1850, and Simon Legree is, for Stowe, the diabolic incarnation of that hideous surrender of Yankee integrity. The last paragraph of the novel, still intense, peals out a prophecy worthy of John Brown himself:

> A day of grace is yet held out to us. Both North and South have been guilty before God; and the *Christian church* has a heavy account to answer. Not by combining together, to protect injustice and cruelty, and making a common capital of sin, is this Union to be saved,—but by repentance, justice and mercy; for, not surer is the eternal law by which the millstone sinks in the ocean, than that stronger law, by which injustice and cruelty shall bring on nations the wrath of Almighty God!

Some critics have remarked that Uncle Tom's Christian forbearance is unpersuasive to them, since it seems more than human. Perhaps the character *is* a touch more than human; there is a biblical grandeur to him that his utterances almost consistently earn. But he is more myth (in the positive sense) than cartoon or caricature, and the book's context sustains his martyrdom. Simon Legree doubtless is more persuasive: He owes something to the Puritan spirit in its decadence and decline, and he has his affinities to that other great devil, Hawthorne's Chillingworth in *The Scarlet Letter.* It is exactly accurate, aesthetically and spiritually, that his greatest hatred for Tom is caused by the slave's overwhelmingly sincere Christianity. The savage gusto of Stowe's villain was caught up splendidly in Vachel Lindsay's "Simon Legree—A Negro Sermon," the first of three poems that he dedicated to the memory of Booker T. Washington. Lindsay's chant concludes with a mad glee that Stowe might not have appreciated, and yet it testifies to the lasting imaginative power that had created Simon Legree:

> And the Devil said to Simon Legree:
>   "I like your style, so wicked and free.
>   Come sit and share my throne with me,
>   And let us bark and revel."
> And there they sit and gnash their teeth,
> And each one wears a hop-vine wreath.
> They are matching pennies and shooting craps,
> They are playing poker and taking naps.
> And old Legree is fat and fine:
> He eats the fire, he drinks the wine—
> Blood and burning turpentine—
> *Down, down with the Devil;*
>   *Down, down with the Devil;*
>   *Down, down with the Devil.* ❖

Biography of Harriet Beecher Stowe

Harriet Elizabeth Beecher was born in Litchfield, Connecticut, on June 14, 1811, the daughter of the Reverend Lyman and Roxana Beecher and sister of Henry Ward Beecher, the celebrated clergyman, author, and editor. She underwent a severe religious upbringing by her stern and tyrannical father, who was a follower of Jonathan Edwards, preaching hellfire and damnation in his thunderous lectures and scorning the female members of his family. Harriet herself, although remaining deeply religious throughout her life, developed a much milder and more benificent Christian temperament. After her mother's death in 1816 she came under the influence of her eldest sister Catherine, who a few years later set up a school in Hartford where Harriet was first a student and later a teacher.

Harriet began writing in the mid-1820s; among her earliest works are a theological essay and an unfinished blank-verse tragedy, *Cleon* (1825). In 1832 the family moved to Cincinnati, Ohio, where Lyman Beecher became president of the Lane Theological Seminary and Catherine Beecher founded a college for women, the Western Female Institute. Harriet was an assistant at the institute until the school closed in 1837. On January 6, 1836, Harriet married Calvin Ellis Stowe, a professor of biblical literature at her father's seminary. They would eventually have seven children; one of them died in the cholera epidemic of 1849 and another was drowned in 1857. Harriet's first publications were stories written for the *Western Monthly Magazine* in 1833; initially her motives for writing were no loftier than to provide money for her family. In 1843 she published *The Mayflower; or, Sketches of Scenes and Characters among the Descendants of the Pilgrims.*

Harriet Beecher Stowe gained her first direct knowledge of slavery while living in Cincinnati. Kentucky, a slave state, lay just across the Ohio River, and Ohioans were divided in their response to runaway slaves, some believing they should be returned to their owners. Both the Beechers and the Stowes were opposed to slavery and eventually joined the abolitionist cause. Harriet and Calvin Stowe once took into their home a little girl who claimed she was free. When her master came to claim her the Stowes helped her escape at night.

In 1850 Stowe moved to Brunswick, Maine, where her husband had been appointed professor at Bowdoin College. There she wrote her antislavery novel *Uncle Tom's Cabin,* serialized in the *National Era* in 1851–52 and published in book form in 1852. The novel was a tremendous success and was translated into at least twenty-three languages. It was, however, violently attacked in the slave-holding South (and also by some newspapers in the North), so in 1853 Stowe published *A Key to* Uncle Tom's Cabin to demonstrate the factual basis for her book. She followed *Uncle Tom's Cabin* with a second antislavery novel, *Dred: A Tale of the Great Dismal Swamp* (1856), based in part on the Nat Turner slave uprising in 1831; but it was very poorly received. As a means of escaping from the vilification she was suffering in the press, Stowe visited Europe in 1853, 1856, and 1859. Her travel impressions were written up in *Sunny Memories of Foreign Lands* (1854).

Uncle Tom's Cabin and the Civil War made Harriet Beecher Stowe a celebrity and her name a household word. When she called on Abraham Lincoln at the White House, he greeted her by saying, "So this is the little lady who made this big war." John William DeForest, writing in the *Nation* in 1868, first used the phrase "The Great American Novel" to describe *Uncle Tom's Cabin.* Stowe, however, did not participate much in the Civil War, although her son Frederick William volunteered on the Union side and was seriously injured at Gettysburg. After the war she wrote a number of sketches of "leading patriots of the day" (all on the Union cause, and including Abraham Lincoln, Frederick Douglass, and her brother Henry Ward Beecher), published as *Men of Our Times* (1868). She also turned her attention to journalism, contributing frequently to the newly founded *Atlantic Monthly.* The association was profitable for both until the publication in 1869 of Stowe's "The True Story of Lady Byron's Life," a sympathetic representation of Lady Byron's separation from the poet and their marital difficulties, including Byron's incestuous relationship with his half-sister. The story lost the magazine 15,000 subscribers and dealt a heavy blow to Stowe's national prestige. Undeterred, she expanded the article to book length and published it as *Lady Byron Vindicated* in 1870.

In 1852 the Stowes had moved to Andover, Massachusetts. After Calvin Stowe's retirement in 1864 from the theological seminary there, the family moved to Hartford, Connecticut. Stowe's novels of this period are chronicles of New England life: *The Minister's Wooing* (1859), *The Pearl of Orr's Island* (1862), *Oldtown Folks* (1869), and *Poganuc People* (1878). From 1868 to 1884 the Stowes spent the winter in Florida, where Harriet assisted in the cause of Reconstruction. Her descriptive sketches of Florida were collected as *Palmetto-Leaves* (1873). She also wrote a number of stories for children (*Queer Little People*, 1867; *Little Pussy Willow*, 1870) and domestic novels (*My Wife and I*, 1871; *Pink and White Tyranny*, 1871; *We and Our Neighbors*, 1875), which elaborate upon some points raised in a treatise she wrote with her sister Catherine, *The American Woman's Home* (1869).

Stowe's neighbor for the last twenty years of her life was Mark Twain, who reported poignantly on her increasing physical and mental deterioration in her later years. Harriet Beecher Stowe died in Hartford on July 1, 1896. ❖

Thematic and Structural Analysis

In the short **preface** to *Uncle Tom's Cabin,* Harriet Beecher Stowe adopts a tendentious authorial voice that marks her novel as a call to reform. In abolitionist diction, highly moral and just as sentimental, Stowe advises the reader that "the object of these sketches is to awaken sympathy and feeling for the African race, as they exist among us," in pre–Civil War America. Slavery is the overarching evil to be eradicated, yet stereotypes of African Americans permeate the text from its first sentence, and the cultural superiority of the "dominant Anglo-Saxon race" is never in question. Through the experiences of various protagonists, the themes of the novel pivot upon a Christian model of suffering and redemption, the acts of the moral individual and the corresponding failure of a democratic society, and the troubling replacement of racist cruelty by racist benevolence. *Uncle Tom's Cabin* is a narrative of its time, but it offers to the modern critical reader insight into the pervasive effects of slavery upon American culture.

In **chapter one** we overhear two Kentucky men negotiating the sale of several slaves, including Uncle Tom and a four-year-old quadroon boy, Harry. Haley, the slave trader, and Mr. Shelby, their owner, are contrasts in appearance and caste. The former is a coarse, obviously prosperous man involved in a perfectly legal, if distasteful, business; the latter is a gentleman who calls himself "humane" and "hate[s] to take the boy from his mother," but must, after all, pay his debts. Haley reminds Mr. Shelby that a critical difference between slaves and "white folks" is that slaves cannot—and do not—expect to keep their wives and children. Stowe tells us that Kentucky has "the mildest form" of slavery and that the apparent ease and stability of slave life may deceive a visitor into believing that slavery is a benign "patriarchal institution."

Harry's mother, Eliza, overhears the slave trader's offer for her son and, astonished and distraught, appeals to her mistress. Mrs. Shelby knows nothing of her husband's financial difficulties, nor can she imagine that he would sell his slaves. She assures Eliza that the sale of Harry is as unthinkable as that of her own children.

In **chapters two and three** Stowe depicts the dependence of the slave family upon those who own them. Eliza, the "petted and indulged favorite" of her mistress, is a gracious, refined, and beautiful mulatto married to George Harris, a mulatto slave on a nearby plantation. And although the couple had been married in the Shelbys' parlor, with "white gloves, and cake and wine," Eliza and George are at the mercy of the whims and indulgences of their owners. George is hired out by his master to work in a factory and invents an agricultural device, which earns him the admiration of his employer and the resentment of his master, who abruptly returns him to the "meanest drudgery" on the farm. Furious over his mistreatment, George reveals to his wife his plans to run away to Canada, where he will work, save money, and buy his family from Mr. Shelby. Unaware that their child has been sold, Eliza, who equates obedience to her master and mistress with Christian commitment, urges him to have faith and forbearance. George has less gentle thoughts, demanding, as if of God, "Who made this man my master?"

Stowe abruptly shifts scenes—as she does frequently in the novel—to Tom and his wife, Chloe, presiding over a humble and "respectable" domesticity within their own cabin on the Shelby plantation (**chapter four**). Tom's African features are "characterized by an expression of grave and steady good sense, united with much kindliness and benevolence." As Chloe cooks dinner he struggles to write, instructed by "Mas'r George," the Shelbys' thirteen-year-old son, and a love of home and of children pervades the slave cabin. Tom is a sort of local religious patriarch: After dinner, slaves arrive from surrounding plantations for worship and singing. At the same time, Mr. Shelby and the slave trader conclude their business in the master's house. Haley assures Shelby he will sell Tom into good hands.

Shelby's debts are cleared, and he informs his wife of the transaction (**chapter five**). She reacts strongly, urging her husband to make "a pecuniary sacrifice" to settle his debt rather than sell Tom and Harry, but he insists that "there is no choice between selling these two and selling everything." Mrs. Shelby resolves to see the slaves in person rather than arrange to be away when they are taken, as her husband suggests.

Eliza overhears the Shelbys' conversation and prepares to run away with her child. She stops at Tom's cabin to tell him that he has been sold and will be taken in the morning. Tom realizes that his value as a slave will be sufficient to save others from being sold and that by running he would doom them all. Eliza asks Tom and Chloe to tell her husband that she will try to reach Canada and meet him there.

Chapter six opens the next morning when the Shelbys discover that Eliza has run off with her child. Mr. Shelby, his honor at stake, rushes off to calm Haley and to offer his horses and servants for a search. With the complicity of Mrs. Shelby, the other slaves—in a rather comical interlude—conspire to hinder the search.

In **chapters seven and eight** maternal love is a powerful force strong enough to overcome desolation, cold, and fierce pursuit. In a scene that would become a literary symbol of female peril and endangerment, Eliza escapes across the Ohio River, literally one step ahead of the slave trader. Shoeless and bleeding, she clutches her child and jumps across huge chunks of broken ice. Throughout the novel slaves endure hardship and danger as a matter of course, but they must redeem themselves out of slavery by extraordinary acts of courage and spiritual strength.

A stranger helps Eliza up the Ohio bank and directs her to a nearby house where fugitive slaves are protected. A "poor, heathenish man," the stranger is impressed by her courage and exclaims that she has earned her liberty. Stowe dryly remarks that had the man been "better situated and more enlightened," he would have known not to assist an escaping slave.

Meanwhile Haley, having been forced to abandon his pursuit of Eliza, takes refuge in a nearby tavern. There he meets his former partner, Tom Loker, and Loker's new partner, Marks. He arranges for the men to catch the escaped mother and child. In payment, they will be "given" Eliza to sell in New Orleans.

In **chapter nine** the divergence of legislative and moral imperatives is evidenced in the passing of the Fugitive Slave Act of 1850, under which the North was no longer a legal haven for runaways and Canada became the closest place of freedom. The reader is introduced to Senator Bird of Ohio, who defends the act to his unsympathetic wife, Mary, claiming that it will keep peace with Kentucky slave owners. Mary vows to break this law at the first opportunity. Although the senator admires her conviction, he makes a distinction between feelings and judgment when political unrest may be alleviated by legal compromise. But the appearance of Eliza and her child, needy and pathetic, appeals more strongly to his moral sense than an abstract, legalistic image of a runaway slave: "[H]is idea of a fugitive was only an idea of the letters that spell the word. . . . The magic of the real presence of distress . . . these [images] he had never tried." Eliza's journey continues as the senator secretly takes her to the home of a man who has freed all his own slaves and now protects others. Senator Bird gives the man money for Eliza and Harry's needs and leaves to resume his legislator's duties in Columbus.

We return to Tom's cabin on the Shelby plantation as he prepares for the arrival of the slave trader (**chapter ten**). Stowe invests Tom with a "gentle, domestic heart," "characteristic of his unhappy race." He knows that this is the last time he will see his children, since few return from the southernmost plantations. Africans, whose "instinctive affections" are "peculiarly strong," whisper in terror among themselves about being "sold south." Escape to Canada requires that the slave overcome a "naturally patient, timid and unenterprising" character. Tom is an anomaly that Stowe defines carefully. Neither fearful nor timid, he is an archetypal passive resister whose eyes are always turned toward God. Honorable in all things, Tom will not ruin his master's credit with the slave trader by running away.

Haley leaves, having shackled Tom to prevent his escape. Young "Mas'r George" catches up to the wagon and vows to come after Tom and bring him back to Kentucky.

Chapter eleven opens in a small country hotel where a traveler, Mr. Wilson, comes across a handbill advertising a reward for the capture or killing of a runaway slave (George Harris). The reader learns that Wilson is the manufacturer to whom George was hired out before his escape. Soon after, a stranger enters the inn and requests a room. Wilson recognizes the man, despite his disguise as a white gentleman of property, as George. Later, in George's quarters, Wilson urges him not to risk his life by breaking the laws of his country. "Sir," George replies, "I haven't any country. . . . But I'm going to have one . . . when I get to Canada, where the laws will own me and protect me, *that* shall be my country." Moved, Wilson offers George money and promises to deliver a token to Eliza when he returns home.

In **chapter twelve** the slave auction concludes, Haley takes Tom and his other human purchases onto a riverboat, and they begin a hellish journey south. Elegant white travelers comment upon the condition of the "Negro"; a clergyman manipulates Scripture to justify slavery; a mother tells her questioning child that although the separation of families is a "bad thing," it doesn't happen often enough to matter, and slaves are better off than they would be if free; a delicate and intelligent young minister predicts that God will bring Haley "into judgment"; a slave drowns herself after the sale of her infant son, and Haley records her death in his account book as a loss. The author interjects with the observation that "the enlightened, cultivated, intelligent" man is as much to blame for tolerating slavery as the trader for dealing in it.

In **chapter thirteen** we learn that Eliza and her child have found shelter in a Quaker settlement in Ohio and that the Quakers are making arrangements to secure their safe passage. While there, they are reunited with George, and they prepare to leave after sundown.

Tom's journey south continues, and he meets the spiritually precocious white child, Evangeline St. Clare (**chapter fourteen**). In the character of Little Eva, as she is called, Stowe concentrates a religious and moral clarity that the text suggests is possible only in children and in the darkest Africans. Eva and Tom become friends after he saves her from drowning, and her father, a Louisiana plantation owner, purchases Tom at her request. The story of Augustine St. Clare and his family, continuing through chapter twenty-nine, describes the effects of a brutal system upon both masters and slaves. St. Clare is an impractical and tenderhearted skeptic, liberal and indulgent with his slaves, his hypochondriac wife, and his daughter. His forty-five-year-old cousin, Ophelia, travels with them from her home in Vermont to look after the delicate Eva and to help manage the household during his wife's frequent illnesses.

Ophelia St. Clare is "a living impersonation of order, method, and exactness." Well read and energetic, she is a firm believer in duty, religion, the abolition of slavery, and the proper training of children. Augustine, Ophelia, Eva, and Tom arrive at the plantation (**chapter fifteen**). Eva rhapsodizes on the beauty of her home, but to Ophelia it seems "old and heathenish." Tom, by his link to a lush and splendid African exoticism, Stowe tells us, is comfortable here. Eva greets "Mammy," a "decent mulatto woman," with repeated kisses, and the affection is returned without restraint. Ophelia remarks to Augustine that she could not kiss a slave as Eva does. In **chapter sixteen** Marie St. Clare, the languid image of decayed, effete Southern attitudes, counters Ophelia's criticism of her having separated Mammy from her husband and children when she married and moved from her father's plantation. "Don't you believe that the Lord made them of one blood with us?" Ophelia asks. "No, indeed, not I!" Marie replies, later elaborating, "And just as if Mammy could love her little dirty babies as I love Eva!" Augustine counters with his distinction between simple love for one's fellow man and the abstract benevolence of the Northern abolitionists: "You loathe them as you would a snake or a toad, yet you are indignant at their wrongs. You would not have them abused; but you don't want to have anything to do with them yourselves."

In **chapter seventeen** preparations continue at the Ohio Quaker settlement to help George and Eliza escape to Canada with their child. Once on their way, they are pursued by traders Loker and Marks. Trapped with their Quaker guide in an isolated range of rocks, the former slaves defend themselves with George's pistols by firing on the party below. Loker is injured and deserted by his party; the fugitives continue their journey after leaving Loker in the care of nearby Quakers.

Like the suicide on the riverboat, another mother is destroyed by loss in **chapter eighteen**. Prue, who brings breads for sale to the St. Clare plantation, is a known drinker. She tells Tom that her life has been spent as a breeder of children who were all sold "as fast as they got big enough." She had hoped to keep the last one but, forbidden by her mistress to feed it, was unable to keep it alive. "I tuck to drinkin', to keep its crying out of my ears! I did,—and I will drink!" she tells Tom, as he tries to comfort her with promises of heaven. Since heaven is "where white folks is gwine," Prue prefers hell. In **chapter nineteen** she dies, locked in a cellar by her master. Ophelia confronts St. Clare about legal protections for the likes of Prue. He replies that there is no law to protect a slave and that the only "resource" is to ignore the excesses of barbarous people.

Chapter twenty introduces Topsy, a neglected, unloved, troublesome young slave girl. Dispensing with any natural attachment to parents or to God, she tells Ophelia, "I spect I grow'd. Don't think nobody never made me." Despite her constant professions of uncontrollable "wickedness," her inept thievery, and some pathological lying, we discover that Topsy is as pure of heart as Little Eva. Dark-skinned, with a "goblin-like" face and twinkling eyes, she retains a sense of self and a peculiar dignity, although her short life has been bereft of love. St. Clare has purchased the girl for Ophelia to mold as she wishes, challenging his cousin to fulfill her Northern abolitionist ideals. Eva and Topsy become friends and playmates.

The scene then shifts to the Shelby plantation, where Tom's wife, Aunt Chloe, is hired out as a baker in Louisville (**chapter twenty-one**). The Shelbys agree to hold her wages toward buying back her husband.

In **chapter twenty-two** we see Tom and Eva again after two years have passed. By this time they have become nearly inseparable and Eva's health has deteriorated from "that soft, insidious disease" that we later learn is tuberculosis. She expresses her wish to free all of her family's slaves and to teach them to read and write, but this idea meets with ridicule from her mother. **Chapter twenty-three** introduces St. Clare's twin brother, Alfred, and his son, Henrique, who have arrived on a visit. Their unrelenting cruelty toward their slaves stands in sharp contrast to Eva's simple love of fellow man and St. Clare's ideal of true democracy.

Eva weakens rapidly and tells Tom and St. Clare that she is dying (**chapter twenty-four**). She implores her father to "go all round and try to persuade people to do right" about slavery, to "have all slaves made free." Eva tells her friend Topsy that Ophelia would love her if only she were good, to which Topsy simply replies, "No; she can't bar me, 'cause I'm a nigger" (**chapter twenty-five**). The ruthless clarity of the child's understanding cuts through the rhetoric of religious ideality and moral sentiment. St. Clare overhears the children and makes a Christian metaphor literal in order to translate Eva's message of love for Ophelia. He reminds his cousin that Christ had put his hands on the blind in order to give them sight. Ophelia admits that she is repulsed by Topsy's touch, yet she imagines, incorrectly, that the child is insensitive to it. "[H]ow can I help feeling so?" she asks. St. Clare speculates that Ophelia, an "old disciple," might learn from Eva, the younger one.

Eva's dying is a long and melodramatic process that evokes the pathos common in deaths by tuberculosis in nineteenth-century novels (**chapter twenty-six**). Her bedroom is filled with objects intended to bring only "heart soothing and beautiful thoughts," and she reads her Bible as much as her failing strength will allow. Topsy brings flowers, and the insufferable Marie cannot understand the affection between the children. Eva again tries, without success, to convince her mother that Topsy is not inherently wicked but has been unloved until now, and that the child wants to be good. Tom spends much time with Eva in her illness. They are kindred spirits, alike in religious faith and in imagination.

The effects of Eva's death are immediate upon the household members (**chapter twenty-seven**). As Topsy mourns the death of the only person who has ever loved her, Ophelia is moved, at last, to love her young student. St. Clare wonders what he may do in response to the lesson of Little Eva's goodness. In his emptiness he turns to Tom and admits that he wants to believe the Bible but cannot. Tom says that he would give his life if it would make "Mas'r" a Christian.

Although religious faith eludes him, St. Clare becomes more practical and circumspect in the management of his slaves and informs Tom that he will emancipate him (**chapter twenty-eight**). Ophelia asks Augustine to make Topsy legally hers, and her cousin reminds her that she will then be a slaveholder and a "backsliding" abolitionist. But Ophelia understands that Topsy must have an owner to protect her and that by owning her she will then be able to bring her to the "free states" and give her liberty. But Topsy's emancipation papers are the only such papers St. Clare completes: He dies soon after, stabbed by a stranger. His master's habitual negligence dooms Tom, as Marie ignores her husband's desire to emancipate him and decides to sell all the slaves but Topsy (**chapter twenty-nine**). Ophelia writes to the Shelbys on Tom's behalf in an effort to save him from auction.

The scene in the slave warehouse, described in **chapter thirty**, is Stowe's most powerful and deftly drawn portrayal of the pervasiveness of the slave trade in America. Human property is valuable, so this New Orleans facility is a neatly kept house where slaves are fed and groomed for market "separately or in lots, to suit the convenience of the purchaser." Stowe carefully describes how the head of a "respectable" Northern firm, having become the creditor of a Southern plantation owner, is compelled to become involved in slave trade to recoup his losses: "He didn't like trading in slaves and souls of men . . . but, then, there were thirty thousand dollars in the case, and that was rather too much money to be lost for a principle."

A refined and "respectably dressed" mulatto woman and her fifteen-year-old quadroon daughter are among the lot to be sold with the St. Clare slaves. Susan and her daughter, Emmeline, have been brought up as Christians. The girl is expected to bring a high price for her beauty, and Stowe compares the mother's feelings to those of "any other Christian mother," except that she will find no refuge in religious or moral principle: The man who will receive the profits for the sale of the two women is a Northerner and a Christian. Susan is bought by a kindly man who tries to buy Emmeline as well, but he is outbid by Simon Legree, who also buys Tom.

The barbarousness with which female slaves in particular were "evaluated" and sold is also plainly evident in Stowe's slave auction scene. Although at the time any African ancestry legally designated one a "Negro," female slaves with traces of European ancestry were prized for their exotic beauty. The scene in which Legree, before the sale, runs his hands appraisingly over Emmeline's body would be outrageous and obscene to polite nineteenth-century readers—except that Emmeline is a slave of racially mixed blood.

Since the publication of *Uncle Tom's Cabin,* Simon Legree's name has, for good reason, become synonymous with evil and cunning. In **chapters thirty-one and thirty-two** Legree and the new slaves arrive at a place of cypress swamps, snakes, mournful wind, and rotting vegetation after a grueling boat trip upriver. Here slaves work without comfort and with only the meanest provisions and shelter. They rise at dawn to pick cotton; they eat at midnight. Still, Tom's faith in God remains unshakable, and in dreams Little Eva reads to him from the Bible. He works diligently in the fields and waits, with "religious patience," for some way of escape.

A strange woman joins the slaves at work in the fields in **chapter thirty-three**. Her delicate features and graceful bearing, good clothing, and scornful pride distinguish her among the ragged and hungry slaves as she picks cotton with fierce speed and skill. The woman, Cassy, initially does not speak but keeps close to Tom, as if sensing his singular strength. Tom helps a weakened woman unable to keep up with the fast pace of the work by filling her sack with his own cotton. Cassy muses that he will abandon all kindness once he realizes how hard it is to take care of himself in this place. "The Lord never visits these parts," she bitterly remarks.

Late in the evening the slaves return to a building where the cotton is weighed and collected by Simon Legree. He offers Tom a promotion to slave driver if he will flog the woman he had helped that day in the field. Tom refuses and Legree violently batters him, asking if the Bible does not order servants to obey their masters. "[M]y soul an't yours, Mas'r," Tom replies. Badly beaten, Tom lies alone in the refuse room of the gin-house, where Cassy comes to care for him (**chapter thirty-**

four). As she tends his wounds and soothes his pain she urges him to give up hope in God. She tells him that she has lived, "body and soul," with Legree for five years and that now he has "a new one," whom the reader already knows as Emmeline. She argues against Tom's hope with the story of her own despair, but he maintains that Legree can really do no more to him than kill him and that Christ's promise of redemption will be fulfilled after death. The believer cannot lose, and Cassy wants desperately to believe. She tells Tom the story of her life as the pampered daughter of a slave owner who, like Augustine St. Clare, had meant to free her but had died suddenly before doing so. Cassy's sordid tale of the betrayal of love and the loss of her children is horribly fascinating—and is an increasingly familiar plight in the novel. Cassy is half-mad with despair, and Tom is her last hope.

In **chapter thirty-five** we witness the intensely superstitious nature of Simon Legree. Presented with a coin and a lock of hair found in a packet tied around Tom's neck when he was flogged, Legree thinks of his kindhearted mother, whom he abandoned to pursue the "boisterous, unruly, and tyrannical" ways of his father. Haunted by this reminder, he burns the lock of hair, which Tom received from Eva before her death, and hurls the coin through a window. Cassy warns Legree to leave Tom alone or he will lose time and money harvesting the cotton (**chapter thirty-six**). Legree, who attempts to force an apology out of Tom without success, vows to exact punishment after the harvest.

Chapter thirty-seven briefly returns to the story of George and Eliza Harris as they reach Canada. The exhilaration of their journey to freedom is mirrored in the renewed hope of liberty that Tom eventually inspires in Cassy. In **chapter thirty-eight**, Tom calms Cassy with his gentle and steadfast spirituality. He observes that, while he has the strength to endure his present servitude, Cassy no longer does. She plans a surprisingly simple escape for herself and Emmeline, whom she has befriended (**chapter thirty-nine**).

The garret of Legree's plantation house is believed haunted since the mysterious death of a slave woman there years ago. Cassy subtly revives and intensifies this belief in the imaginations of the slaves and Legree. So when she and Emmeline disappear, everyone believes that they have either escaped or have perished in the swamp, and the noises heard in the garret, where the two are actually hiding, only confirm belief in the ghosts. From her hiding place Cassy witnesses the martyrdom of Tom (**chapter forty**). He refuses to reveal what he knows of the women's disappearance and is beaten severely by Legree and two slaves who have been made, by manipulation and abuse, to betray and torment their fellow slaves. The "savage men" repent, weeping and asking Tom to tell them about Jesus. Christ-like, Tom forgives them.

In **chapter forty-one** young George Shelby, having received Ophelia's letter, at last locates Tom and intends to buy him back in fulfillment of his promise. He arrives too late to save him, but not too late to comfort his old friend at his death. Tom counsels forgiveness as he dies, and even Legree seems momentarily awed by his persistent faith and his saintliness. George vows to God that he will do everything he can to "drive out this curse of slavery." That night Cassy and Emmeline leave the plantation, and slaves will later speak of having seen two white figures "gliding" upon the road (**chapter forty-two**). Disguised as a Creole woman and her servant, they board a riverboat headed north.

In the same chapter we learn of a string of coincidences uniting many of the novel's characters in familial relationships long severed by slavery. A woman on the boat reveals the existence of Cassy's long-lost daughter—who, we learn, is Eliza (**chapter forty-three**). The woman, whose master had freed her, married her, and left her a fortune upon his death, is George Harris's sister. All are reunited in Canada, where the Harris household becomes a place of education, refinement, and family love.

In **chapter forty-four** Chloe and the Shelbys learn of Tom's death from George Shelby. Now the master of his father's plantation, George frees all the slaves, promising them fair wages should they decide to stay on. He attributes his change of heart to the courageous life and brutal death of Tom.

As the extended family of George Harris makes plans to emigrate to Liberia, the reader senses the author's perplexity over the future of race relations in a Christian democracy that has yet to abolish slavery. Through the character of George, Stowe suggests that the hope for true freedom may be possible only in another country. "[W]hat can I do for [my enslaved brethren] here?" George asks, in a letter to a friend. "[L]et me go and form part of a nation, which shall have a voice in the councils of nations, and then we can speak." He continues:

> We *ought* to be free to . . . rise by our individual worth . . . and they who deny us this right are false to their own professed principles of human equality. . . . We have *more* than the rights of common men;—we have the claim of an injured race for reparation. But, then, *I do not want it;* I want a country, a nation, of my own.

In **chapter forty-five** Stowe asserts in her own voice that many of the characters and incidents in the novel are based on actual people and occurrences. She acknowledges the troubling responsibility that will arise with the end of slavery: "Does not every American Christian owe to the African race some effort at reparation for the wrongs that the American nation has brought upon them?" Skeptical that justice to former slaves is possible in a nation in which the slave trade is firmly entrenched, Stowe suggests that the best way to make amends is to assure that the emancipated slave is provided an education before returning to Africa. She concludes with a resounding call to "repentance, justice and mercy" on the part of both Northern and Southern Americans, invoking the "wrath of Almighty God" on those who will not heed this call to save the Union.

Despite its melodramatic style, *Uncle Tom's Cabin* is an immensely moving novel and a social document of American culture. Harriet Beecher Stowe struggles, not altogether unconsciously, against her own racism as she attacks, with passion, a truly evil institution. By appealing to sentiment, evoking an emotional identification with the slave, and counseling a more Christ-like interpretation of Scripture, Stowe may convince the modern reader that, if slavery was not the issue that caused the Civil War, it should have been. ✤

—Tenley Williams
New York University

List of Characters

Uncle Tom, a slave, is a figure of Christ-like suffering and endurance. He is a loving husband and father, an honorable man in a dishonorable society. A model of passive resistance, he draws his strength from his unquestioning faith in the Christian promise of a better life to come. For Tom, the present is explicable only as a part of God's greater vision, so he patiently accepts the misery of his life and the lives of the slaves around him, without hope of social reform. His religious strength comforts those who suffer as it awakens in his oppressors a recognition of God's mercy and a fear of his retribution. He dies a martyr's death, refusing to betray two escaped slaves.

George and Eliza, although slaves on separate plantations, marry and have a son. The family stays together only through the clemency and the financial stability of their masters, and when Eliza learns that her son is to be sold, she flees north. George is reunited with the family, and they eventually establish a home in Canada. The desire for political dialogue and power ultimately motivates George to move his family to Liberia, a new African nation with modern ideals.

Evangeline St. Clare—"Little Eva"—is the precocious daughter of a slave owner. A kindred soul to Tom, she is a figure of spiritual purity. Like Tom, she believes that Christ will deliver all into a better life after death and that the task of both slaves and slave owners is to work to earn this reward. Eva dies of consumption, and her exemplary life motivates all who know her to emulate her kindness and compassion.

Augustine St. Clare is a slave owner whose beliefs are poised between the Northern and Southern viewpoints. He understands both the pretensions of abolitionist ideality and the cancerous corruption of slavery in the plantation system. He is kind and generous to his slaves and is both bemused and spiritually overwhelmed by his power over their lives. His self-confessed flaw is his laziness, and St. Clare's weakness of character costs his slaves their freedom, and, in Tom's case, his life: St. Clare dies before implementing his promise to emancipate him.

Ophelia St. Clare is Augustine's cousin, brought from Vermont to oversee his household and the care of Eva. She is an organized, well-read, sensible abolitionist who is nonetheless repulsed by the thought of touching a "Negro." Through Eva's example of racially blind love, she experiences an epiphany at Eva's death that inspires in her a capacity to love her young charge, Topsy.

Marie St. Clare, the mother of Little Eva, is a self-absorbed hypochondriac incapable either of loving or of being loved, though Eva tries. She is irredeemably racist, and—by ignoring her husband's final wish to emancipate him—she proves instrumental in Tom's doom.

Topsy, a slave girl, is the most startling and arguably the most charming character in the novel. Raised as though she were livestock, she has never known parents, family, or love, yet Topsy is as pure of heart as Little Eva. St. Clare purchases Topsy for Ophelia, challenging her to practice her Northern moral precepts and spiritual pretensions with a child who has known nothing of God or of family life. She is acutely aware of Ophelia's disgust at her touch and articulates her perceptions without equivocating. She and Little Eva become friends and, after Eva's death, Topsy's inherent goodness wins Ophelia's love.

Simon Legree is the corrupt and brutal plantation owner who buys Tom after the death of Augustine St. Clare. A spiritually barren man, he is ruled by his appetites and superstitions. Through him Stowe alludes to the sexual servitude of young slave women and girls in the figures of the tragically betrayed Cassy and the morally imperiled Emmeline. Legree beats Tom to death.

Cassy is the slave mistress of Simon Legree, sent to work the fields when he replaces her with Emmeline, a young girl purchased at auction. The daughter of a slave mother and a wealthy and loving slave holder who meant to free her legally, the once-beautiful Cassy is refined and graceful. Alternately embraced by the white world and abandoned to slavery, she had lived a life of privilege with a white master in whose love she had trusted. But he abandoned her and their children, selling them all into slavery, and Cassy is filled with despair. She is drawn to Tom because of his spiritual strength. His stoic endurance restores Cassy's hope, and with Emmeline she escapes to Canada and is reunited with her long-lost daughter Eliza. ✤

Critical Views

[*Uncle Tom's Cabin* was violently attacked by many different parties and for a variety of reasons; one of the criticisms concerned the seeming unreality of the characters. In *A Key to* Uncle Tom's Cabin (1853), Stowe defends the book and, in the following excerpt, maintains that the character of Uncle Tom was drawn from several black slaves she knew personally.]

The character of Uncle Tom has been objected to as improbable; and yet the writer has received more confirmations of that character, and from a great variety of sources, than of any other in the book.

Many people have said to her, "I knew an Uncle Tom in such-and-such a Southern State." All the histories of this kind which have thus been related to her would of themselves, if collected, make a small volume. The author will relate a few of them.

While visiting in an obscure town in Maine, in the family of a friend, the conversation happened to turn upon this subject, and the gentleman with whose family she was staying related the following. He said, that when on a visit to his brother in New Orleans, some years before, he found in his possession a most valuable negro man, of such remarkable probity and honesty that his brother literally trusted him with all he had. He had frequently seen him take out a handful of bills, without looking at them, and hand them to this servant, bidding him go and provide what was necessary for the family, and bring him the change. He remonstrated with his brother on this imprudence; but the latter replied that he had had such proofs of this servant's impregnable conscientiousness that he felt it safe to trust him to any extent.

The history of the servant was this. He had belonged to a man in Baltimore, who, having a general prejudice against all the religious exercises of slaves, did all that he could to prevent his having any time for devotional duties, and strictly forbade him to read the Bible and pray, either by himself or with the other servants; and because, like a certain man of old, named Daniel, he constantly disobeyed this unchristian edict, his master inflicted upon him that punishment which a master always has in his power to inflict—he sold him into perpetual exile from his wife and children, down to New Orleans.

The gentleman who gave the writer this information says that, although not a religious man at the time, he was so struck with the man's piety, that he said to his brother, "I hope you will never do anything to deprive this man of his religious privileges, for I think a judgment will come upon you if you do." To this his brother replied that he should be very foolish to do it, since he had made up his mind that the man's religion was the root of his extraordinary excellences. ⟨. . .⟩

In the town of Brunswick, Maine, where the writer lived when writing *Uncle Tom's Cabin,* may now be seen the grave of an aged coloured woman, named Phebe, who was so eminent for her piety and loveliness of character, that the writer has never heard her name mentioned except with that degree of awe and respect which one would imagine due to a saint. The small cottage where she resided is still visited and looked upon as a sort of shrine, as the spot where old Phebe lived and prayed. Her prayers and pious exhortations were supposed to have been the cause of the conversion of many young people in the place. Notwithstanding that the unchristian feeling of caste prevails as strongly in Maine as anywhere else in New England, and the negro, commonly speaking, is an object of aversion and contempt, yet so great was the influence of her piety and loveliness of character, that she was uniformly treated with the utmost respect and attention by all classes of people. The most cultivated and intelligent ladies of the place esteemed it a privilege to visit her cottage; and when she was old and helpless, her wants were most tenderly provided for. When the news of her death was spread abroad in the place, it excited a general and very tender sensation of regret. "We have lost Phebe's prayers," was the remark frequently made afterwards by members of the church, as they met one another. At her funeral, the ex-governor of the State and the professors of the college officiated as pall-bearers, and a sermon was preached, in which the many excellences of her Christian character were held up as an example to the community. A small religious tract, containing an account of her life, was published by the American Tract Society, prepared by a lady of Brunswick. The writer recollects that on reading the tract, when she first went to Brunswick, a doubt arose in her mind whether it was not somewhat exaggerated. Some time afterwards she overheard some young persons conversing together about the tract, and saying that they did not think it gave exactly the right idea of Phebe. "Why, is it too highly coloured?" was the inquiry of the author. "Oh, no, no, indeed!" was the earnest response; "it doesn't begin to give an idea of how good she was."

Such instances as these serve to illustrate the words of the Apostle, "God hath chosen the foolish things of the world to confound the wise; and God hath chosen the weak things of the world to confound the things which are mighty."

—Harriet Beecher Stowe, *A Key to* Uncle Tom's Cabin (1853; rev. ed. Boston: John P. Jewett Co., 1854), pp. 37–38, 40–41

SAMUEL WARREN ON *UNCLE TOM'S CABIN* AS AN AGENT OF SOCIAL CHANGE

[Samuel Warren (1807–1877), a British novelist, critic, and physician, wrote a number of technical legal works, many reviews, and several novels. In this review of *Uncle Tom's Cabin,* Warren praises the authenticity of the work but questions whether it will have any actual effect as a political tract.]

Uncle Tom's Cabin is a remarkable book unquestionably; and, upon the whole, we are not surprised at its prodigious success, even as a mere literary performance; but whether, after all, it will have any direct effect upon the dreadful INSTITUTION at which it is aimed, may be regarded as problematical. Of one thing we are persuaded—that its author, as she has displayed in this work undoubted genius, in some respects of a higher order than any American predecessor or contemporary, is also a woman of unaffected and profound piety, and an ardent friend of the unhappy black. Every word in her pages issues glistening and warm from the mint of woman's love and sympathy, refined and purified by Christianity. We never saw in any other work, so many and such sudden irresistible appeals to the reader's heart—appeals which, moreover, only a wife and a mother could make. One's heart throbs, and one's eyes are suffused with tears without a moment's notice, and without anything like effort or preparation on the writer's part. We are, on the contrary, soothed in our spontaneous emotion by a conviction of the writer's utter artlessness; and when once a gifted woman has satisfied her most captious reader that such is the case, she thenceforth leads him on, with an air of loving and tender triumph, a willing captive to the last. There are, indeed, scenes and touches in this book which no living writer, that we know of, can surpass, and perhaps none even equal.

No English man or woman, again, could have written it—no one, but an actual spectator of the scenes described, or one whose life is spent with those moving among them; scenes scarce appreciable by FREE English readers—fathers, mothers, husbands, wives, brothers and sisters. We can hardly *realise* to ourselves human nature tried so tremendously as, it seems, is only adumbrated in these pages. An Englishman's soul swells at the bare idea of such submission to the tyrannous will of man over his fellowman, as the reader of this volume becomes grievously familiar with; and yet we are assured by Mrs Stowe that she has given us only occasional glimpses of the indescribable horrors of slavery. To this part of the subject, however, we shall return. Let us speak first, and in only general terms, of the literary characteristics of the author, as displayed in her work.

Mrs Stowe is unquestionably a woman of GENIUS; and that is a word which we always use charily: regarding genius as a thing *per se*—different from talent, in its highest development, altogether, and in kind. Quickness, shrewdness, energy, intensity, may, and frequently do accompany, but do not constitute genius. Its divine spark is the direct and special gift of God: we cannot completely analyse it, though we may detect its presence, and the nature of many of its attributes, by its action; and the skill of higher criticism is requisite, in order to distinguish between the feats of genius and the operations of talent. Now, we imagine that no person of genius can read *Uncle Tom's Cabin,* and not feel in glowing contact with genius—generally gentle and tender, but capable of rising, with its theme, into very high regions of dramatic power. This Mrs Stowe has done several times in the work before us—exhibiting a passion, an intensity, a subtle delicacy of perception, a melting tenderness, which are as far out of the reach of mere talent, however well trained and experienced, as the prismatic colours are out of the reach of the born blind. But the genius of Mrs Stowe is of that kind which instinctively addresses itself to the Affections; and though most at home with the gentler, it can be yet fearlessly familiar with the fiercest passions which can agitate and rend the human breast. With the one she can exhibit an exquisite tenderness and sympathy; watching the other, however, with stern but calm scrutiny, and delineating both with a truth and simplicity, in the one case touching, in the other really *terrible.*

"*Free* men of the North, and Christians," says she, in her own vigorous and earnest way, "cannot know *what slavery is.* . . . From this arose a desire," on the author's part, "to exhibit it in a *living dramatic reality.* She has endeavoured to show it fairly in its best and its worst phases. In its *best* aspect, she has perhaps been successful; but oh! who shall say what yet remains untold in that *valley and shadow of death* that lies on the other side? . . . . The writer has only given a faint shadow—a dim picture—of the anguish and despair that are at this very moment riving thousands of hearts, shattering thousands of families, and driving a helpless and sensitive race to frenzy and despair."

—Samuel Warren, [Review of *Uncle Tom's Cabin*], *Blackwood's Edinburgh Magazine* No. 456 (October 1853): 395–96

J. W. DeForest on the Search for the Great American Novel

[J. W. DeForest (1826–1906), a historian and novelist, is the author of *History of the Indians of Connecticut* (1853) and *Miss Ravenel's Conversion from Secession to Loyalty* (1867), a Civil War novel. In this extract, DeForest argues that *Uncle Tom's Cabin,* despite its flaws, could be classified as the closest approximation to the "great American novel" because of its breadth of purpose and depth of feeling.]

According to   J W deforest,

The nearest approach to the desired phenomenon "the great American novel" is *Uncle Tom's Cabin.* There were very noticeable faults in that story; there was a very faulty plot; there was (if idealism be a fault) a black man painted whiter than the angels, and a girl such as girls are to be, perhaps, but are not yet; there was a little village twaddle. But there was also a national breadth to the picture, truthful outlining of character, natural speaking, and plenty of strong feeling. Though comeliness of form was lacking, the material of the work was in many respects admirable. Such Northerners as Mrs. Stowe painted we have seen; and we have seen such Southerners, no matter what the people south of Mason and Dixon's line may protest; we have seen such negroes, barring, of course, the impeccable Uncle Tom—uncle of no extant nephews, so far as we know. It was a picture of American life, drawn with a few strong and passionate strokes, not filled in thoroughly, but still a portrait.
　　—J. W. DeForest, "The Great American Novel," *Nation,* 9 January 1868, p. 28

(Bloom 31)

❖

Charles F. Richardson on Some Reasons for the Success of *Uncle Tom's Cabin*

[Charles F. Richardson (1851–1913) wrote *The Choice of Books* (1900) and *American Literature 1607–1885*

(1887–89), from which the following extract is taken.
Here, Richardson argues that the success of *Uncle
Tom's Cabin* rests on Stowe's ability to create sympathetic and realistic characters and on her willingness to
leaven her serious intent and melodramatic style with
passages of humor.]

In the far cold North, where her husband was at the time a professor in Bowdoin College, Mrs. Stowe looked toward the sun-
lit South, and beheld beneath fair skies all the horror of the
wide-spread and blighting evil of human slavery, with its curs-
es of lust and lash, broken homes and bleeding hearts; hate
and cruelty and greed on the one hand, and the dogged
endurance of hopeless woe on the other. The horrible system of
slavery was not unmitigated by occasional kindness; many a
freedman has sincerely said that sorrow and suffering never
came until abolition severed him from the old master and mistress, and threw him all unfit upon the world, with a ballot in
his hand but no wisdom in his brain. Yet no question of past
political expediency, no consideration, even, of exaggeration in
the book, as regards the average condition of the negroes in
the Southern States, can blind our eyes to the essential and
enduring success of the novel. It is far from faultless in development of plot, delineation of character, or literary style; but it
strongly seizes a significant theme, treats it with immediate
originality and inevitable effect, and meanwhile adds several
individual characters to the gallery of fiction. It was everywhere
an anti-slavery argument because its pictures of episodes in the
history of slavery were so manifest and so thrilling. Read in
every state of the North and in parts of the South, and translated into twenty languages of Europe, it aroused the indifferent
and quickened the philanthropic. Its power was felt, perhaps
unconsciously, before a quarter of its pages had been read.

The author of "Uncle Tom's Cabin" had the wisdom—not
possessed by the pessimistic or self-blinded delineators of later
woes in Russia—to brighten her pages by touches of humor
and kindly humanity, and to obey the canons of the novelist's
art as well as those of the moralist's conscience. Thereby her
force was quadrupled, for literature both popularizes and per-
petuates morality, while morality without art is fatal to litera-

ture. The book remains a vivid panorama of people and scene in a bygone time, now remanded by final war to a past that must ever be historic and can never be repeated. The "abolition of tribal relations in Christ" was the broad theme of a Christian woman; and in treating it she produced an art-result of such inherent merit that the hand helped the soul as much as the soul the hand.

—Charles F. Richardson, *American Literature 1607–1885*
(New York: Putnam's, 1887–89), Vol. 2, pp. 410–12

CHARLES EDWARD STOWE ON SOME TRUE INCIDENTS BEHIND STOWE'S FICTION

[Charles Edward Stowe (b. 1850), the son of Harriet Beecher Stowe, compiled an important biography of his mother from her journals and letters (1889). In an extract from that work, Stowe tells how an actual incident involving an escaped slave led in part to the writing of *Uncle Tom's Cabin*.]

In 1839 Mrs. Stowe received into her family as a servant a colored girl from Kentucky. By the laws of Ohio she was free, having been brought into the State and left there by her mistress. In spite of this, Professor Stowe received word, after she had lived with them some months, that the girl's master was in the city looking for her, and that if she were not careful she would be seized and conveyed back into slavery. Finding that this could be accomplished by boldness, perjury, and the connivance of some unscrupulous justice, Professor Stowe determined to remove the girl to some place of security where she might remain until the search for her should be given up. Accordingly he and his brother-in-law, Henry Ward Beecher, both armed, drove the fugitive, in a covered wagon, at night, by unfrequented roads, twelve miles back into the country, and left her in safety with the family of old John Van Zandt, the fugitive's friend.

It is from this incident of real life and personal experience that Mrs. Stowe conceived the thrilling episode of the fugitives' escape from Tom Loker and Marks in *Uncle Tom's Cabin.*
—Charles Edward Stowe, *Life of Harriet Beecher Stowe Compiled from Her Letters* (Boston: Houghton, Mifflin, 1889), p. 93

BRANDER MATTHEWS ON STOWE'S FAIRNESS

[Brander Matthews (1852–1929) was an important American critic, editor, and novelist. He wrote many volumes, including *An Introduction to the Study of American Literature* (1896) and *The Development of the Drama* (1903). In this extract, Matthews comments that Stowe was fair in her portrayal of Southerners, since she blamed the institution of slavery and not individuals.]

The smoke of the war has cleared away now and the heat of combat has died down; and as one reads the book with unimpassioned eye, it is easy to understand why Mrs. Stowe thought that she had dealt so fairly with the southern people that they would not be offended. As we read it now we see that the indictment of the system was so damning that those who accepted slavery could not but denounce the book and declare it detestable. While proving that slavery itself was black and foul and hideous, the authoress was perfectly fair to the slaveholders themselves, showing that it was the system which was bad and not the individual. The most offensive, brutal, hardened character in the book is Simon Legree—and he is a New Englander. The pleasantest and most welcome character in the book is St. Clare—and he is a native southerner: indeed it may be questioned whether the new southern novelists, skilful as they are and understanding their fellow southerners as they do, have as yet given us any portrait of the southern gentleman as charming as Mrs. Stowe's St. Clare, as easy, as good-humored, as quick-witted, as kindly, as keen, as lazy, or as true to life itself. The contrast between St. Clare and Legree forces itself on every reader, however careless; and with a due sense of climax the dark figure comes last.

Even the careless reader today will see that the story straggles not a little and lacks firm structure; it bears evidence that it was written from week to week, without a settled plan, and that it grew on the author's hands almost in spite of herself. As Mrs. Stowe told the publisher, "the story made itself, and that she could not stop till it was done." The tale was nearly half told before the need for "comedy relief," as the playmakers phrase it, led to the introduction of Topsy, perhaps the most popular figure in the book; and it was drawing to its close before we were made acquainted with Cassy, perhaps the most picturesque character in the story and certainly not the least true. The intensity of the author's feeling was so keen, her knowledge of her subject was so wide, her unconscious and intuitive artistic impulse was so vigorous, that she shaped her story so as best to accomplish its purpose, building better than she knew and doing more than she dared to hope.

—Brander Matthews, "American Fiction Again," *Cosmopolitan* 13, No. 3 (March 1892): 637

THOMAS WENTWORTH HIGGINSON ON SOME CRITICISMS OF *UNCLE TOM'S CABIN*

[Thomas Wentworth Higginson (1823–1911), an important American critic, is the author of *Short Studies of American Authors* (1880), *Hints on Writing and Speech-Making* (1898), and *Contemporaries* (1899). He was the first editor of the poems of Emily Dickinson (1891). In this extract, Higginson takes note of some criticisms, especially from Southerners, of *Uncle Tom's Cabin*.]

A further question has sometimes been raised as to how far the book was correct in its pictures of slavery. One result of this debate was to induce Mrs. Stowe to publish, in 1853, a *Key to Uncle Tom's Cabin*, giving chapter and verse, so to speak, for every incident she had employed. It is certain that many

Southerners of high standing, beginning with Senator Preston of South Carolina—in a conversation with Prof. Lieber—admitted that every fact it contained might be duplicated from their own observation. All this might be true, however, and yet the general atmosphere of such a book might be unfair; there might be unfairness also in the omissions. It is stated by Mrs. Stowe herself that she expected more criticism from the abolitionists than from the slaveholders themselves. Perhaps the keenest criticism ever made upon *Uncle Tom's Cabin* was from a Southern lady who, while conceding the probable truth of all the incidents, complained that Mrs. Stowe had described neither the best nor the worst class of slaveholders. Those who could not accept Legree as a sufficient approach to the latter type must have had a terrible experience. As to the former, it is enough to say that Mrs. Stowe was consciously engaged upon an anti-slavery tract, not, like Frederick Law Olmsted, in an economic study; and that the very impotence of the more humane slaveholders either to emancipate their slaves or to extricate themselves from the toils of the system, is not the least weighty part of the indictment against American slavery.

—Thomas Wentworth Higginson, "Harriet Beecher Stowe," *Nation,* 9 July 1896, p. 25

FRED LEWIS PATTEE ON STOWE AND DICKENS

[Fred Lewis Pattee (1863–1950) was a prominent scholar of American literature. He wrote *Side Lights on American Literature* (1922), *The Development of the American Short Story* (1923), and *The First Century of American Literature 1770–1870* (1935). In this extract, Pattee likens the techniques used by Stowe to make an argument for social change to the techniques used by Charles Dickens, maintaining that both writers appealed chiefly to the emotions rather than to the intellect.]

Her attack upon slavery was not obvious. She did not preach and she did not argue and she made no frontal attack. Like

Dickens, she aroused emotion; she created characters that her reader could feel as if they were present in the room. The victims were under-dogs, and in America they were therefore to be pitied. The oppressors were all utter villains. The novel came in the one moment in history when it would have been received as a world classic. For America was tense with emotion, and that emotion was almost as intense in Europe, especially in England. As a period novel it had every element that would make for popularity: it was melodramatic, with a hero and heroines and villains; it was sentimental even to the Dickens extremes; it had humor of the Jim Crow type; it had negro spirituals sung by slaves; and it had a strong religious motif such as could come only from one reared, as she had been, in such an atmosphere as she was later to present in her *Oldtown Folks.*

Dickens with his *Pickwick* and his *Oliver Twist* and the novels that followed undoubtedly created a new reading public. Hostlers and weavers and servant girls who never before had thought of books as things to be read laughed over Sam Weller and the fat boy and cried when Paul Dombey died and Little Nell. In the same way *Uncle Tom's Cabin* enlarged greatly the American reading public. For one thing it broke down a long stretch of the stockade that had guarded Puritan families from the "contagion" of novels, long believed in Christian homes to be works inspired by the devil. Everybody read *Uncle Tom.* Was it not history? Was it not a weapon against slavery? Was not Mrs. Stowe saying that the hand of God held her hand as she wrote it? And they followed it into the theater and saw Little Eva go up to Heaven on a wire which they did not see, with "not a dry eye in the house." They saw Eliza cross the ice with her baby in her arms and the awful bloodhounds leaping at her throat, and they went home shuddering at the death of Uncle Tom ready to canonize him as a veritable saint. Surely uncounted thousands went to see a Tom drama who never before had seen the inside of a theater.

—Fred Lewis Pattee, *The Feminine Fifties* (New York: D. Appleton-Century, 1940), pp. 137–38

[James Baldwin (1924–1987), an important black
American novelist, was also an occasional critic.
Among his works of nonfiction are *Notes of a Native
Son* (1955), *Nobody Knows My Name* (1961), and *The
Evidence of Things Not Seen* (1985). In this extract
from his celebrated essay on *Uncle Tom's Cabin*,
Baldwin argues that Stowe's work is not so much a
novel as an abolitionist tract and that it is a failure as a
work of fiction.]

Uncle Tom's Cabin is a very bad novel, having, in its self-
righteous, virtuous sentimentality, much in common with *Little
Women*. Sentimentality, the ostentatious parading of excessive
and spurious emotion, is the mark of dishonesty, the inability to
feel; the wet eyes of the sentimentalist betray his aversion to
experience, his fear of life, his arid heart; and it is always, therefore, the signal of secret and violent inhumanity, the mask of
cruelty. *Uncle Tom's Cabin*—like its multitudinous, hard-boiled
descendants—is a catalogue of violence. This is explained by
the nature of Mrs. Stowe's subject matter, her laudable deter-
mination to flinch from nothing in presenting the complete picture; an explanation which falters only if we pause to ask
whether or not her picture is indeed complete; and what constriction or failure of perception forced her to do so depend on
the description of brutality—unmotivated, senseless—and to
leave unanswered and unnoticed the only important question:
what it was, after all, that moved her people to such deeds.

But this, let us say, was beyond Mrs. Stowe's powers; she
was not so much a novelist as an impassioned pamphleteer;
her book was not intended to do anything more than prove
that slavery was wrong; was, in fact, perfectly horrible. This
makes material for a pamphlet but it is hardly enough for a
novel; and the only question left to ask is why we are bound
still within the same constriction. How is it that we are so loath
to make a further journey than that made by Mrs. Stowe, to
discover and reveal something a little closer to the truth?

⟨. . .⟩ The figure from whom the novel takes its name, Uncle
Tom, who is a figure of controversy yet, is jet-black, wooly-

haired, illiterate; and he is phenomenally forbearing. He has to be; he is black; only through this forbearance can he survive or triumph. (Cf. Faulkner's preface to *The Sound and the Fury:* These others were not Compsons. They were black:—They endured.) His triumph is metaphysical, unearthly; since he is black, born without the light, it is only through humility, the incessant mortification of the flesh, that he can enter into communion with God or man. The virtuous rage of Mrs. Stowe is motivated by nothing so temporal as a concern for the relationship of men to one another—or, even, as she would have claimed, by a concern for their relationship to God—but merely by a panic of being hurled into the flames, of being caught in traffic with the devil. She embraced this merciless doctrine with all her heart, bargaining shamelessly before the throne of grace: God and salvation becoming her personal property, purchased with the coin of her virtue. Here, black equates with evil and white with grace; if, being mindful of the necessity of good works, she could not cast out the blacks—a wretched, huddled mass, apparently, claiming, like an obsession, her inner eye—she could not embrace them either without purifying them of sin. She must cover their intimidating nakedness, robe them in white, the garments of salvation; only thus could she herself be delivered from ever-present sin, only thus could she bury, as St. Paul demanded, "the carnal man, the man of the flesh." Tom, therefore, her only black man, has been robbed of his humanity and divested of his sex. It is the price for that darkness with which he has been branded.

—James Baldwin, "Everybody's Protest Novel," *Partisan Review* 16, No. 6 (June 1949): 578–79, 581

CHARLES H. FOSTER ON THE MERITS OF *UNCLE TOM'S CABIN*

[Charles H. Foster (b. 1913) taught at the University of Iowa, Grinnell College, and the University of Minnesota. He has edited *Emerson's Theory of Poetry* (1939) and *The Rungless Ladder* (1954), a book on Stowe from which the following extract is taken. Here,

Foster ponders the merits of Stowe's novel: It bears relations with the work of James Fenimore Cooper and Mark Twain and anticipates later fiction by southerners, especially William Faulkner.]

Uncle Tom's Cabin belongs to a lower species than the American masterworks of the 1850's: *The Scarlet Letter, Moby-Dick, Walden,* and *Leaves of Grass.* As writer, Harriet stands close to that other important regional novelist, James Fenimore Cooper, who died the year before *Uncle Tom's Cabin* appeared as a book. Like Cooper, she did not see her way to the destruction of the conventional novel and the creation of a new form appropriate to her new subject matter. Like him, she continued in broad outlines the tradition of the sentimental novel. George and Eliza have much of the rhetorical unreality of similar characters in Cooper and, if we remember the incident of the slave catchers, they are even involved in an approximation of Cooperesque flight and pursuit with the woodsman in the form of Phineas Fletcher thrown in for good measure. But much more significant is the similarity between *Uncle Tom's Cabin* and *The Pioneers,* for example, in their true centers of interest. In Natty Bumppo and Uncle Tom, Harriet and Cooper were not seeking to create myth; they were simply projecting against the American landscape figures larger than life who stalked their imaginations. Something closely resembling myth resulted, however, in both instances. As Natty Bumppo popularly became the archetypal frontiersman ever in conflict with civilization, so Uncle Tom became the archetypal American Negro, exploited by the white man and sold South symbolically again and again. Uncle Tom is still a figure who can move us as we read. In our concentration on the truly artistic mythmaker, Melville, we are likely to underrate Harriet's achievement. Criticism must eventually recognize her, I believe, as a major mythmaker to the populace throughout the world.

Once we grant the importance of Uncle Tom as myth is there any other aspect of Harriet's first novel which may hold our attention on the literary level? Uncle Tom appears overidealized when we compare him with Jim in *Huckleberry Finn,* and Lucy and Cassy fare only slightly better when we compare them with Roxana in *Pudd'nhead Wilson.* But, as I have indicated, Sam, Marks, and Dinah would not be out of place in

Mark Twain's St. Petersburg and Dawson's Landing. These characters, together with Miss Ophelia and her Vermont friends and relations, by fits and starts bring us into a vigorously conceived American world.

It is possible also that some readers of fiction will be intrigued by Harriet's anticipation of Faulkner, Caldwell, and other contemporary Southern writers. Faulkner's objective correlative to his awareness of the curse brought to the South by slavery is one of the major works of the American imagination. Harriet's St. Clare family appears paper-thin by comparison; but the Sutpens, the Sartorises, the Compsons are more clearly implied in Alfred St. Clare, his son Henrique, and Augustine's wife, Marie, than in characters of any earlier American book. Perhaps the most striking foreshadowing of Faulkner is the denouement of the novel. In terms of his legend, as it is brought down to modern times, there is something almost prophetic in the fact that Uncle Tom, the Negro, who was not freed by his noble but ineffective master, becomes the property of a man embodying the greed, the vulgarity, the lust, the Inhumanity which outrage Faulkner as he broods over the South following the heroic days.

—Charles H. Foster, *The Rungless Ladder: Harriet Beecher Stowe and New England Puritanism* (Durham, NC: Duke University Press, 1954), pp. 59–61

EDMUND WILSON ON THE "ERUPTIVE FORCE" OF *UNCLE TOM'S CABIN*

[Edmund Wilson (1895–1972) was perhaps the leading American literary critic of his age. Among his many works are *The Wound and the Bow* (1947), *Axel's Castle: A Study in the Imaginative Literature of 1870–1930* (1931), and *Patriotic Gore* (1962), a landmark work on Civil War literature from which the following extract is taken. Here, Wilson claims that Stowe's novel has not received the attention it deserves and goes on to praise its "eruptive force" and skillful characterization.]

To expose oneself in maturity to *Uncle Tom* may therefore prove a startling experience. It is a much more impressive work than one has ever been allowed to suspect. The first thing that strikes one about it is a certain eruptive force. This is partly explained by the author in a preface to a late edition, in which she tells of the oppressive silence that hung over the whole question of slavery before she published her book. "It was a general saying," she explains, "among conservative and sagacious people that this subject was a dangerous one to investigate, and that nobody could begin to read and think upon it without becoming practically insane; moreover, that it was a subject of such delicacy that no discussion of it could be held in the free states without impinging upon the sensibilities of the slave states, to whom alone the management of the matter belonged." The story came so suddenly to Mrs. Stowe and seemed so irresistibly to write itself that she felt as if some power beyond her had laid hold of her to deliver its message, and she said sometimes that the book had been written by God. This is actually a little the impression that the novel makes on the reader. Out of a background of undistinguished narrative, inelegantly and carelessly written, the characters leap into being with a vitality that is all the more striking for the ineptitude of the prose that presents them. These characters—like those of Dickens, at least in his early phase—express themselves a good deal better than the author expresses herself. The Shelbys and George Harris and Eliza and Aunt Chloe and Uncle Tom project themselves out of the void. They come before us arguing and struggling, like real people who cannot be quiet. We feel that the dams of discretion of which Mrs. Stowe has spoken have been burst by a passionate force that, compressed, has been mounting behind them, and which, liberated, has taken the form of a flock of lamenting and ranting, prattling and preaching characters, in a drama that demands to be played to the end.

Not, however, that it is merely a question of a troubled imagination and an inhibited emotional impulse finding vent in a waking fantasy. What is most unexpected is that, the farther one reads in *Uncle Tom,* the more one becomes aware that a critical mind is at work, which has the complex situation in a very firm grip and which, no matter how vehement the characters become, is controlling and coördinating their interrelations. Though there is much that is exciting in *Uncle Tom's Cabin,* it is never the crude melodrama of the decadent phase of the play; and though we find some old-fashioned moralizing and a couple of Dickensian deathbeds, there is a good deal less sentimentality than we may have been prepared for by our memories of the once celebrated stage apotheosis—if we are old enough to have seen it: "Little Eva in the Realms of Gold." We may even be surprised to discover that the novel is by no means an indictment drawn up by New England against the South. Mrs. Stowe has, on the contrary, been careful to contrive her story in such a way that the Southern states and New England shall be shown as involved to an equal degree in the kidnapping into slavery of the Negroes and the subsequent maltreatment of them, and that the emphasis shall all be laid on the impracticability of slavery as a permanent institution. The author, if anything, leans over backwards in trying to make it plain that the New Englanders are as much to blame as the South and to exhibit the Southerners in a favorable light ⟨. . .⟩

—Edmund Wilson, "Harriet Beecher Stowe," *Patriotic Gore: Studies in the Literature of the American Civil War* (New York: Oxford University Press, 1962), pp. 5–7

ALICE C. CROZIER ON *UNCLE TOM'S CABIN* AS POLEMIC

[Alice C. Crozier is a professor of English at Rutgers University in New Brunswick, New Jersey. She is the author of *The Novels of Harriet Beecher Stowe* (1969), from which the following extract is taken. Here, Crozier argues that *Uncle Tom's Cabin* is a polemic not so much against the South as against the educated citizens of the North and South who allowed the system of slavery to develop and continue.]

It is no news to anyone that *Uncle Tom's Cabin* is a polemic. Nevertheless, it is useful to clarify the grounds of the argument, and, lest it still be supposed by some that *Uncle Tom's Cabin* is an anti-Southern book, to identify just who is being attacked. This can most readily be done by studying the many references in the novel to the Declaration of Independence and the subjects Mrs. Stowe associates with it. It is also natural to inquire into the remedies, proposed or implied, to which the polemic leads; these are conveyed most clearly through the novel's sentimental heroine, little Eva, and secondarily by the words and example of that "moral miracle," Uncle Tom.

The argument is often introduced by a scene or picture. The strategy is illustrated by one of the scenes on the boat which is taking Uncle Tom from Kentucky to New Orleans. Among the slaves whom Haley has brought and is taking to market is a young woman named Lucy with a baby, whom Haley sells to a man on the boat. The man explains that his " 'cook lost a youn 'un last week,—got drownded in a wash-tub, while she was a hangin' out clothes,—and I reckon it would be well enough to set her to raisin' this yer.' " Haley steals the baby while Lucy is asleep and sells him. Mrs. Stowe expects the reader's wrath to rise at this tale, and she quickly points the moral.

> The trader that arrived at that stage of Christian and political perfection which has been recommended by some preachers and politicians of the north, lately, in which he had completely overcome every humane weakness and prejudice. . . . The wild look of anguish and utter despair that the woman cast on him [when she discovered the sale] might have disturbed one less practised; but he was used to it. He had seen that same look hundreds of times. You can get used to such things, too, my friend; and it is the great object of recent efforts to make our whole northern community used to them, for the glory of the Union.

For the glory of the Union! The ogre, then, is Daniel Webster. Who is to blame? Webster, yes, but also "you" dear reader who allow yourself to rejoice in the glory of the Union.

Mrs. Stowe never makes a point just once. Several pages later, when Haley discovers that the woman has jumped overboard and drowned herself, we are told that Haley's response was to consider himself an ill-used man, decidedly; but there was no help for it, as the woman had escaped into a state which *never will* give up a fugitive,—not even at the demand of the whole glorious Union. . . .

'He's a shocking creature, isn't he,—this trader? so unfeeling! It's dreadful, really!'

'O, but nobody thinks anything of these traders! They are universally despised,—never received into any decent society.'

But who, sir, makes the trader? Who is most to blame? The enlightened, cultivated, intelligent man, who supports the system of which the trader is the inevitable result, or the poor trader himself? You make the public sentiment that calls for his trade, that debauches and depraves him, till he feels no shame in it; and in what are you better than he?

Thus it is the system itself that is evil, and its most corrupt members are neither the trader nor the slaveholder but rather the pious, educated, respectable citizenry of North and South who self-righteously despise the brutish trader but who are too smug and too selfish to disturb their own complacency on behalf of reform. The polemic attacks the reader.

—Alice C. Crozier, *The Novels of Harriet Beecher Stowe* (New York: Oxford University Press, 1969), pp. 7–9

NOEL B. GERSON ON STOWE'S CONCEPTION OF CHRISTIANITY

[Noel B. Gerson (1914–1988) is the author of many biographies, including those of Pocahontas (1973), the Marquis de Lafayette (1976), and Harriet Beecher Stowe (1976), from which the following extract is taken. Here, Gerson discusses Stowe's conception that slavery could not exist in a truly Christian world.]

During the long months of writing—and for the rest of her life—Mrs. Stowe remained convinced she had written a moderate work, consonant with her religion and the teachings of her father. Her Kentucky family, the Shelbys, were kind and civilized and treated their slaves with compassion. But they, like the slaves themselves, were victims of the institution itself, and it was that institution, its injustices magnified by the cruelties of the cold-blooded, inhumane slave trade, that she sought to expose and destroy.

In a truly Christian world, she believed, slavery could not exist. Its perpetuation was partly the fault of the churches, including the conservative wing of the Presbyterian movement. These organizations had lost sight of two basic tenets: that God's love is all-pervasive and that man redeems himself through Christ. Instead of practicing religion, they had allowed themselves to become enmeshed in hair-splitting theological arguments, while the wicked and the evils they perpetrated flourished.

At no time did the author's common sense desert her. Her slave-owner characters, in the main, are decent, honorable people, themselves victims of the institution of slavery and more commendable than the abolitionists who advocated any means, no matter how violent, to rid the nation of a curse. More radical antislavery elements in the country, she predicted in her correspondence, would be "sorely disappointed" by her book and might even regard her as a traitor to their cause.

She was also concerned with what would become of the former slaves should immediate, complete emancipation be granted. No longer would there be a place for them on the plantations of the South. Illiterate, without the skills that would enable them to work in the factories, they would not be at home in the rapidly industrializing North either, particularly as most Northern citizens, despite their professed antislavery sentiments, were showing no tendency to admit blacks into their homes, their schools, or even their churches. To send all the freed slaves to Liberia, a plan advocated by many abolitionists, struck her as absurd: Their only hope for the future lay on the road to Christianity, and in Africa they would revert to heathenism. Though Mrs. Stowe's opposition to slavery had hardened, she still clung to the opinion that gradual emancipation achieved through religion and education provided the only genuine solution. The economy of the South would be disrupted when the slaves departed, and gradual emanicipation was the only fair way to protect plantation owners, who would need time to find other sources of labor.

Apparently unable to assess the intensity of feeling in both North and South, Mrs. Stowe believed that in writing her book she was performing a healing function. Extremists might hate her, but *Uncle Tom's Cabin* would surely appeal to moderates in both sections of the country; when they banded together, slavery could be destroyed in the manner least harmful to everyone concerned.

—Noel B. Gerson, *Harriet Beecher Stowe: A Biography* (New York: Praeger, 1976), pp. 68–69

ELIZABETH AMMONS ON STOWE'S EXTOLLING OF MOTHERHOOD

[Elizabeth Ammons is a professor of English at Tufts University and the author of *Edith Wharton's Argument with America* (1980) and *Conflicting Stories: American Women Writers at the Turn into the Twentieth Century* (1991). In this extract, Ammons studies Stowe's belief that she was chosen to write *Uncle Tom's Cabin* because she was a woman and a mother.]

Late in the nineteenth century Harriet Beecher Stowe announced that God wrote *Uncle Tom's Cabin* (1852). The novel by then seemed too monumental even to its author to have been imagined by one woman. Earlier in her life, in contrast, Stowe had no doubt that she wrote the subversive book or that she was inspired to write it, despite marital and household irritations, precisely because she was a woman.

In a letter to her husband ten years before the publication of the novel, and almost ninety years before Virginia Woolf's famous declaration of independence on behalf of all women writers in *A Room of One's Own* (1929), Harriet Beecher Stowe said: "There is one thing I must suggest. If I am to write, I must have a room to myself, which shall be *my* room." With her room came the mission to write what became America's best-known novel, and the mission fell to her, she believed, because she was a mother. She recalled for one of her grown children, "I well remember the winter you were a baby and I was writing 'Uncle Tom's Cabin.' My heart was bursting with the anguish excited by the cruelty and injustice our nation was showing to the slave, and praying God to let me do a little and to cause my cry for them to be heard. I remember many a night weeping over you as you lay sleeping beside me, and I thought of the slave mothers whose babies were torn from them." One of her seven children died while still an infant. She says: "It was at his dying bed and at his grave that I learned what a poor slave mother may feel when her child is torn away from her." Authors' remarks on the genesis of their work sometimes prove misleading, but not in this case. Stowe's insistence on maternal experience as the generative principle of *Uncle Tom's Cabin* identifies the ethical center of the novel, and helps explain the unusual, and often misunderstood, characterization of Tom.

Stowe's protagonist is gentle, pious, chaste, domestic, long-suffering and self-sacrificing. In a nineteenth-century heroine, those attributes would not seem strange. Associate them, however, with the hero of an American novel, a genre sifted for its Adamic rebels, and readers' complacence can evaporate. Indeed, the farther *Uncle Tom's Cabin* has moved in time from the historical reality of chattel slavery, the more obvious and the more criticized "effeminate" Tom has become; and whether it is stated in so many words or not, often what is objected to is the fact that Stowe makes him a heroine instead of a hero. ⟨. . .⟩

Stowe's treatment of maternal values may at a glance look unremarkable. Nearly every page of *Uncle Tom's Cabin* hymns the virtues of Mother, the revered figure whose benign influence over domestic life in the nineteenth century was conveniently supposed, and promoted, to redress the abuses against humanity engendered in the masculine, money-making realm. Stowe, however, refuses to appoint Mother the handmaiden of Mammon in *Uncle Tom's Cabin*. Instead, she enlists the cult of motherhood in the unorthodox cause of challenging, not accommodating, the patriarchal status quo. Like her sister Catharine Beecher, Harriet Beecher Stowe displays in *Uncle Tom's Cabin* a facility for converting essentially repressive concepts of femininity into a positive (and activist) alternative system of values in which woman figures not merely as the moral superior of man, his inspirer, but as the model for him in the new millennium about to dawn.

—Elizabeth Ammons, "Heroines in *Uncle Tom's Cabin*," *American Literature* 49, No. 2 (May 1977): 161–63

Ann Douglas on Stowe as Feminist

[Ann Douglas (b. 1942), a professor of English at Columbia University, has written *The Feminization of American Culture* (1977) and *Terrible Honesty: Mongrel Manhattan in the 1920s* (1995). In this extract, Douglas maintains that Stowe represented a powerful voice not only for the abolition of slavery but for the advancement of women.]

The multifaceted question of *Uncle Tom's* greatness is not a trivial or irresolvable one. To put it simply, *everything* involved in the writing and in the subject matter of *Uncle Tom's Cabin* was controversial: Stowe's sex, or more specifically, the proper limits of style and material that members of her sex should observe as authors; slavery and racism as religious and political issues; and the form proper to the American novel in contrast with its English counterpart.

Stowe was the most prominent member of what was only the second generation of American women novelists, and the first of their number to attain literary distinction. By 1815 England had already produced Maria Edgeworth, Fanny Burney, and Jane Austen; well flanked by a host of talented minor feminine writers, they established the fact that English women could write novels and even help determine the novel's scope and form. No American women authors of the period can justly be placed in their company. In the late 1930s and 1940s, the English critic F. R. Leavis began his influential discussion of the "great tradition" of the English novel, starting with Austen. In 1923 D. H. Lawrence, brilliantly establishing the legitimacy of "Classic American Literature" in his study of the same name, took James Fenimore Cooper as his first novelist (Cooper started to publish in 1820); Lawrence did not include a single woman writer in the course of a survey that ended with Whitman. While the second generation of Lawrence's chosen (male) authors of American classics—Poe, Hawthorne, Melville, Dana, and Whitman—were writing in the 1840s, 1850s, and 1860s, Dickens and Thackeray were at work in England. But so were the Brontës and George Eliot; indeed, George Eliot is the pivotal figure in Leavis's attempt to define the English novel in its major phase in *The Great Tradition.*

Whether or not Leavis or Lawrence were altogether right in their choices or their analyses, one fact is clear: by 1850, when Harriet Beecher Stowe began *Uncle Tom,* English women were writing profitably and well; American women were writing, at best, profitably. For many reasons they were more rigidly confined by conventional stereotypes of femininity than were their English counterparts. Where English women writers took male noms de plume, such as Currer Bell and George Eliot, American authoresses adopted pretty, alliterative, ultrafeminine floral aliases plainly intended to disarm criticism and disavow ambition. "Fanny Fern" and "Grace Greenwood" could not insist to their readers, as Charlotte Brontë did, that they came before their audience "as author[s] only." Never lacking in energy, the American women by and large stuck to the themes of piety, deference, and domesticity prescribed for their sex. Harriet Beecher Stowe, however, was a correspondent of George Eliot's and a friend of Elizabeth Barrett Browning's, and she deserved to be. She always wrote under her own name and took up whatever subject matter compelled her. Lawbreaking was one of the major themes of her first two novels, *Uncle Tom's Cabin* and *Dred,* and she shared this fascination not with her feminine literary peers but with Hawthorne and Melville.

Stowe was not a declared feminist, although the link between antislavery and the women's movement was a vital one. Women's antislavery groups were formed as auxiliaries to the men's antislavery organizations in the early and mid-1830s. As their members grew more conscious of the discrimination that their male cohorts exercised against them, these all-female groups became the seedbed of the feminist crusade of the late 1840s and 1850s. Stowe—eccentric, moody, dreamy, and energetic by turns—was a maverick; she shied away from all associations and all labels. Yet *Uncle Tom's Cabin,* in its inception, style, and substance, is a powerfully feminist book.

> —Ann Douglas, "Introduction: The Art of Controversy," *Uncle Tom's Cabin* (New York: Penguin, 1981), pp. 11–13

Thomas F. Gossett on the Reception of *Uncle Tom's Cabin*

[Thomas F. Gossett (b. 1916) is a former professor of English at Trinity University in San Antonio, Texas, and the author of a landmark work on racism, *Race: The History of an Idea in America* (1963). In this extract from his exhaustive study of the reception of *Uncle Tom's Cabin,* Gossett concludes that the reactions to Stowe's novels over the years are an index of the prevalence of racism in this country.]

To read the opinions of *Uncle Tom's Cabin* which have been expressed over the past 130 years is something like examining a history of racism in America for this period, at least racism as it has been applied to blacks. J. C. Furnas was right when he said that *Uncle Tom's Cabin* was like a three-stage rocket—it was first powerful as a novel, then as a play, and eventually in the twentieth century as a film. It is doubtful that any work of American literature has received such a variety of interpretations, both in the reviews and criticisms it has generated and in the many ways in which it has been adapted as a play. When the novel was published in 1852, even northern reviewers in surprisingly large numbers criticized it for what they felt were exaggerated accounts of the evils of slavery. Nevertheless, it is obvious that Stowe's book was a powerful force in changing the minds of white northerners and in alerting opinion abroad to the evils of American slavery.

For a long time the almost universal detestation of *Uncle Tom's Cabin* prevented all but a few readers in the South from examining it from any point of view except that of its alleged unfairness to the South and to slavery. When the Civil War was over and the white South had time to calm down, readers and critics there discovered that the novel contained ideas about blacks which might be used to suggest a more sympathetic interpretation of their own view of history. With a little judicious manipulation, many of these white southern interpreters convinced themselves that they could find in *Uncle Tom's Cabin* itself sufficient evidence to justify their own conviction that blacks ought not to have a status in society equal to that of whites. They did not wish to return to slavery, but neither did they wish to give the blacks full rights as citizens. The white South eventually came to admit, at least by implication, that slavery had been wrong, disunion had been wrong, and therefore the South's decision to initiate the Civil War had been wrong. On the other hand, they reasoned, it did not follow that the antebellum white South had been wrong in its belief in the inherent inferiority of blacks.

In the late nineteenth and early twentieth centuries, a substantial number of white northern critics of *Uncle Tom's Cabin* had also changed their opinions and had moved closer to those held by white southerners. A view frequently expressed, especially after northern disillusion with the Reconstruction of the South, was that slavery had been an evil institution and Stowe had been right to indict it. On the other hand, a surprisingly large number of white northern critics came to think Stowe had been wrong in making the black characters in her novel too noble, amiable, and intelligent to be credible. If these critics had said that her black characters generally had better qualities than people of any race, they might have had a point. Usually, however, they merely said that her black characters were presented as being better than real blacks.

In the last forty years, the current of opinion toward Stowe and *Uncle Tom's Cabin* falls chiefly into three categories. Black critics and scholars strongly reject the novel, deploring the frequent recourse to racist explanations of the traits of the characters, especially those of the blacks. A great many white critics—probably a majority—also reject the novel but principally because they find it almost wholly lacking in literary merit. There is a third group, however, who have something like the enthusiasm of earlier critics for both the author and her book. Nearly all of these critics are white, and to those who reject the novel on literary grounds, these critics say that Stowe's faults are a matter of style rather than of substance. They argue that while she used the form of the sentimental and domestic novel, she was able to transcend that form because she had a broad grasp of human nature and was able to analyze both institutions and individual characters with great insight. To the black critics who deplore the novel, the white critics who admire it generally concede that it contains serious faults in its interpretation of the black characters. They argue, however, that Stowe's racism belongs to her time and place. They see her as struggling, and with considerable success, to free herself from it. Properly understood, they argue, the racism is not sufficient to invalidate the novel, and they conclude that Stowe was able not merely to analyze slavery perceptively but to present credible characters, black and white, reacting to a monstrous institution.

—Thomas F. Gossett, Uncle Tom's Cabin *and American Culture* (Dallas: Southern Methodist University Press, 1985), pp. 409–11

JOHN R. ADAMS ON *UNCLE TOM'S CABIN* AS A VICTORIAN NOVEL

[John R. Adams (b. 1900) is the author of critical studies of Edward Everett Hale (1977) and Harriet Beecher Stowe (1963); the following extract is taken from a revised (1989) edition of the latter work. Here, Adams believes that *Uncle Tom's Cabin* was, to its original readers, not a political tract but a story in the sentimental Victorian tradition.]

Only a child can read *Uncle Tom's Cabin* without preconceptions. William Dean Howells, aged fourteen, read it under ideal conditions, week by week, as a serial story by an unknown author. Each chapter was fresh, the picture was clear, the reader could not know what would come next or how the story would end. Above all, the original *Uncle Tom's Cabin* serial was a story, not a controversy. It induced its readers—a special interest group—to weep a lot, laugh a little, become indignant, and perhaps even resolve to lead a better life. As a brand new book, however, offered to the nation and the world, it reached a hostile as well as a sympathetic audience, becoming at once a document with political implications. Over the years it has been the most discussed book in American history, and by now no person who reads it or, certainly, writes about it can see it with the fresh approach of Howells and other enthusiastic readers of the *National Era*. Every synopsis is an analysis, every chapter a question.

What is *Uncle Tom's Cabin* about? To the original readers it was about slavery in the South, a story about weak and wicked people, strong and virtuous people, from fiends to saints. It pleaded for the end of slavery, with the narrator often speaking to the reader, making herself a character in the story. With emancipation accomplished and the original purpose attained (though not in the way Stowe had intended or foreseen) new readers have discovered other themes of enduring importance: family life, racial differences, the superiority of women, personal and social redemption. The meaning of *Uncle Tom's Cabin* has become as debated as its factual accuracy was contested when Stowe wrote it as a description of the life of its time.

Yet the book is a story, no matter how many messages it carries, and the substance could be compressed into a paragraph for some technical purposes, the design is so easily stated. It is one of the Victorian novels in which, according to a common practice, the adventures of two groups of characters are alternated to give an inclusive picture of society and to provide a variety of emotional appeal.

—John R. Adams, *Harriet Beecher Stowe* (Boston: Twayne, 1963; rev. 1989), pp. 24–25

[Josephine Donovan (b. 1941), a professor of English at the University of Maine, is the author of *Feminine Literary Criticism: Explorations in Theory* (1975), *Feminist Theory: The Intellectual Traditions of American Feminism* (1985), and a study of *Uncle Tom's Cabin* (1991), from which the following extract is taken. Here, Donovan examines the theme of evil in the novel and the different characters' responses to it.]

Masterpiece literature also often provides a rich variety and depth of characterization; it often presents a dense, detailed, and convincing sense of reality—whether psychological reality, an epic sense of setting, or the complexities of moral life; and finally, it must have an underlying architectonic integrity—that is, it must exhibit throughout an inherent design, or what Aristotle called *dianoia* or thought.

Uncle Tom's Cabin satisfies these criteria. First, it engages in serious, universal themes. The central issue in the novel is slavery, but Stowe clearly views slavery as a specific manifestation of the problem of evil. Therefore, while the institution of slavery has been abolished, the novel retains its relevance today because the broader issue of the existence of political evil and suffering remains. Indeed, ⟨. . .⟩ it is because of its unflinching examination of this issue that the novel bears a haunting contemporaneity for the twentieth-century reader. It still works to enlarge our moral understanding.

Through her characters Stowe presents a series of possible responses to the moral issue of the existence of evil. George Harris, for example, a slave who escapes north, takes an essentially atheistic approach, saying that a benevolent God would not permit such atrocities as slavery to exist; Uncle Tom takes a Christian approach, that suffering is redemptive and that evil will be atoned for; the slave woman Cassy believes that violence is the only means by which evil can be vanquished; Mrs. Shelby, the Kentucky plantation mistress, and a number of Quakers who operate on the underground railway advocate nonviolent resistance and personal acts to alleviate suffering; St. Clare, a relatively benign plantation owner, counsels an apathetic stance, saying there is nothing one can do to end suffering and oppression. In short, Stowe develops a range of responses to the issue of evil, and her development of them, as we shall see, is done at a level of great moral sophistication.

Second, even a superficial reading of the novel reveals the richness and variety of Stowe's characterization. This is indeed one of her great strengths as a writer. Over a hundred characters are fully developed—from every class and from several regions, including free and slave blacks, northern and southern whites. Similarly, the epic scope of the novel, the range of its settings, and the prodigious detail of its realism provide the reader with an unrivaled sense of the texture of nineteenth-century American life.

Finally, Stowe's novel is carefully constructed according to an identifiable moral architecture. Few critics have recognized the powerful organizing design that undergirds the work. Stowe conceived *Uncle Tom's Cabin* as an *argument* against slavery; it is constructed according to a rhetorical pattern of moral antithesis. It proceeds by means of a series of antithetical characters or sets of characters, building dialectically to the climactic, allegorical final scenes in which Uncle Tom, who has assumed the status of a Christ figure, contends with Simon Legree, the Antichrist. The powerful confrontation between the two, in which Tom endures physical death but gains a spiritual triumph ("the sharp thorns became rays of glory"), brings Stowe's work to an effective moral and formal resolution.

We read *Uncle Tom's Cabin* today through an overlay of twentieth-century atrocities—the Nazi concentration camps, the Soviet gulags, Hiroshima, My Lai. In an era when torture of resisting political prisoners is not uncommon, Uncle Tom's refusal to capitulate to Legree's torture as well as his refusal to engage in violence take on new meaning.

—Josephine Donovan, Uncle Tom's Cabin: *Evil, Affliction and Redemptive Love* (Boston: Twayne, 1991), pp. 12–13

[Jennifer L. Jenkins, at the time she wrote the following article, was a Ph.D. candidate at the University of Arizona. Here, Jenkins asserts that, although Stowe proclaims the ideal of motherhood in *Uncle Tom's Cabin,* the actual mothers in the novel dominate their families by fear, not love.]

Stowe insists in *Uncle Tom's Cabin* that the divisive culture and politics of mid-nineteenth-century America are merely symptoms of a troubled family. Preoccupied with home and family in her own life, she proposes these two forces as common elements in both black and white life in her fictional antebellum South. In *American Woman's Home* (1869) she would promote a domestic separation of labor, in which men build houses and women oversee the households: "The family state then, is the aptest earthly illustration of the heavenly kingdom, and in it woman is its chief minister. . . . To man is appointed the out-door labor." Woman, the "chief minister," rules this domestic heaven, while man is expelled from the maternal "kingdom" to the world of work. Male guilt for abandoning religion and family in favor of trade, according to Barbara Welter, produced this ministerial ideal of the feminine: "He could salve his conscience," she argues, "by reflecting that he had left behind a hostage, not only to fortune, but to all the values which he held so dear and treated so lightly. Woman, in the cult of True Womanhood presented by the women's magazines, gift annuals and religious literature of the nineteenth century, was the hostage in the home." This "cult of True Womanhood" or "cult of domesticity" idealized a pious indoor life of refinement and efficiency designed to please the master, and to transform the mistress into an "angel in the house."

Like any cult, however, domesticity had its dangers. Though the house could symbolize inherited identity for a man, for a woman it often threatened identity itself. With the rise of manufacturing and city-based industry, women, who had once shared pioneer life out-of-doors with men, increasingly were sent to their rooms. For women writers, in particular, the house became an utterly other sort of icon. Built by father, brother or husband, the house could soon prove prison, madhouse, seraglio, or charnel house to its female inhabitants. By the nineteenth century, the enclosure of frontier forests had given way to equally oppressive walls and roofs. Small wonder, then, that houses could become places of some distaste and horror in the female imagination. In *Uncle Tom's Cabin* domestic confinement produces uncanny tendencies both in houses and in the women who run them. So, while Stowe subscribes to contemporary sentimental ideologies of domesticity, her novel actually posits domestic space as a gothic site.

As in most domestic novels, mothers are the agents of power in *Uncle Tom's Cabin.* Stowe contends polemically that motherly love is sacred, demonstrated in pity, tenderness, and prayers—an argument consistent with her image of a domestic heaven. Appropriating this trope, Jane Tompkins has argued that *Uncle Tom's Cabin* offers to "reorganize culture from a woman's point of view," and thus becomes a feminine hagiography of sorts: "It is the *summa theologica* of nineteenth-century America's religion of domesticity, a brilliant redaction of the culture's favorite story about itself—the story of salvation through motherly love. Out of the ideological materials at their disposal, the sentimental novelists elaborated a myth that gave women the central position of power and authority in the culture." This good, Christian mother is the maternal type that Tompkins has found to be a compelling icon in American culture. Indeed, Stowe herself attributed such motherliness to women of all classes and races.

Yet the mothers of *Uncle Tom's Cabin* appropriate this position of authority not by means of love, but of fear. As Julia Kristeva notes, the Christianized notion of maternal love offers "the whole range of love-types from sublimation to asceticism and masochism." One loving, harmless mother does appear in the novel: the Quaker Rachel Halliday. She stands as the cultural ideal of motherhood against which all other mothers in the novel may be measured. When Stowe's women deviate from this benign stereotype they become gothic images of the feminine, and degenerate into extremes: either the madwoman-vampire, or the self-sacrificing mamma who obsessively loves her children to death. The good mothers become particularly horrible, due to the suffocating intensity of their maternal love.

The effect of this ambivalent maternal force is sameness: the vampire and the angel become indistinguishable. From Mrs. Shelby to Mrs. Legree, Stowe's mothers neglect, deceive, or abuse their offspring. As the plot of the novel moves the characters from one mother to the next, an encyclopedia of domestic collapse takes shape. Angelic but insidious mammas meet the underground railroad, while the river journeys on the Mississippi and the Red carry Tom from termagant to shrew to madwoman. Such domestic disruption and collapse fractures the plot and subverts the narrative of *Uncle Tom's Cabin.*

—Jennifer L. Jenkins, "Failed Mothers and Fallen Houses: The Crisis of Domesticity in *Uncle Tom's Cabin,*" *ESQ* 38, No. 2 (Second Quarter 1992): 162–64

GLADYS SHERMAN LEWIS ON PURITAN GENRES AND THE STRUCTURE OF *UNCLE TOM'S CABIN*

[Gladys Sherman Lewis is a professor of English at the University of Central Oklahoma and the author of *Message, Messenger, and Response* (1994), a study of *Uncle Tom's Cabin* from which the following extract is taken. Here, Lewis argues that the novel is based upon several literary genres from the Puritan age, including the sermon and the propaganda tract.]

Puritan genres provide a selection of forms which have accepted conventions in their literary treatment. By manipulating and rearranging several Puritan conventions, Harriet Beecher Stowe transformed in *Uncle Tom's Cabin* the ways in which antebellum America perceived slavery and viewed that culture. Her strategies allow her to articulate social protest, illustrate a social problem, illuminate both the inner and outer context of characters affected by both the protest and the problem of slavery, propose individual and group resolutions, and issue a national call for social change based on these results. Sermon as genre carries the social protest; the captivity narrative defines the social problem; the spiritual autobiography, confessions, and conversion narratives furnish the effect of slavery on the characters and serve to illustrate their resolutions; and jeremiad rhetoric charges the nation to make a response to the issue which influences every individual. By providing the form and proposing the content for the protest against slavery in American culture, the Puritan genres in *Uncle Tom's Cabin* shape both a master design and a master plot which Stowe proposes to the audience as ways to join in a collaboration against the mutual social problem. The design comes from her Christian vision for the world; the plot develops from the stories of people in that world. Although *Uncle Tom's Cabin* draws upon Puritan literary conventions, its content does not, but that practice is conventional in itself because it fits the Puritan pattern of using cultural, human material to deal with the spiritual.

Her novel's master design has three basic parts which are always assumed from any of the sermonic characteristics and must be understood as a divine triad which structures the master plot of the characters. Time is forward moving and based in history which is shaped by Christian millenial eschatology; heaven is the home of the soul and the ideal place; and trinitarian interdependence and mutuality in the Godhead provide a model for ideal human relationships. The complex biblical base which permeates the book with specific citations, allusions, and illustrations in the depiction of characters and in characters's descriptions of themselves and each other consistently point to this three-part scheme which serves to reflect the novel.

In the first part of the paradigm, Stowe holds to a Genesis-creation with time proceeding on a line to its end: "He shall not fail nor be discouraged / Till He have set judgment in the earth" (Isaiah 42:4). After the biblical fall from grace, Christ, the redeeming sacrifice sent by God, the Father, descends into the world to return in ascension, assuring the security of time in historical reality which proceeds in a linear direction to an apocalyptic judgment and beyond for eternity: "I am the resurrection and the Life; he that believeth in me, though he were dead, yet shall he live" (John 11:25).

The second part of her design emphasizes that the soul has a place of destination during its travels through life: heaven as ultimate home. No matter what happens in experience, the hope for heaven as perfect home and rest remains constantly before the soul: "Let not your heart be troubled. In my Father's house are many mansions. I go to prepare a place for you" (John 14:21–22).

The last segment concerns the interaction of mutually distinct spheres in power, love, and activity among the Trinity that forms her ideal for relationships which grant feeling and ethical behavior: "Father, forgive them, for they know not what they do" (Luke 23:34). With a circular movement that travels in both directions, God, the Father, giver of law, order, system, and Old Testament revelation, communicates with God, the Son, Jesus Christ, who personifies grace, love, redemption, and New Testament ethics, and relates to God, the Holy Spirit, the paraclete, enabling believers to enact the New Testament liberty from the law through loving obedience to the ethical demands of faith.

The Christian Trinitarian model for relationships proscribes the love and morality encountered by characters as they move through time and pause in different geographical settings where, while exposed to feelings, they learn morality. Stowe's mental habits reflect Puritan Ramist logic. She constantly balances expressions of opposites: power/submission, bond/free, public/private, aggression/tenderness, dominance/nurture. In human relational paradigms, she arranges people in families as units both of individuals and groups which enact mutually affirming dichotomies of power/weakness, male/female, bond/free, and public/private.

In *Uncle Tom's Cabin* the sermon and the propaganda tract act in tandem with the conflict produced from accounts of captivity narratives, spiritual autobiographies, confessions, and conversion narratives. Sermon structures carry both the law, as its characteristics appear in its various parts through the book, and the protest, as a jeremiad against slavery in its entirety; captivity narratives present the problem; spiritual autobiographies and confessions describe the process of confronting slavery in its many shapes; conversion provides resolutions of the conflicts to propose that one feel right, act right, and do right; and the propaganda tract reinforces the legitimacy of the resolution as a viable solution for the protest presented by the problem and its processes. As a jeremiad, the sermon diagnoses the illness as slavery; the Puritan narratives show how to treat it; and the sermon as propaganda tract presents the prognosis as Stowe argues for the adaptations and adjustments which she considers to be viable solutions. The sermon controls the form of the novel by its use of the Bible through citation and allusion, character typologies, and structure and style of the text. As lay sermons, the captivity narratives restate the master design's ideology in light of individual experience. Spiritual autobiographies and confessions, as stories of conflict with perverted law which has supplanted ideal rule, propose the culture's master plot, that of a nation of people who are exemplary because they internalize the governance and behavior of the master design. Individual conversion narratives implement the sermon's master design and validate the master plot of a nation converted to justice and morality to be God's light to the world in a new covenant where love and feeling in moral codes are more important than doctrine.

> —Gladys Sherman Lewis, *Message, Messenger, and Response: Puritan Forms and Cultural Reformation in Harriet Beecher Stowe's* Uncle Tom's Cabin (Lanham, MD: University Press of America, 1994), pp. 13–16

Works by
Harriet Beecher Stowe

Primary Geography for Children (with Catherine Beecher).
1833.

A New England Sketch. 1834.

*The Mayflower; or, Sketches of Scenes and Characters among
the Descendants of the Pilgrims.* 1843.

Uncle Tom's Cabin; or, Life among the Lowly. 1852. 2 vols.

Earthly Care, a Heavenly Discipline. 1852.

The Two Altars; or, Two Pictures in One. 1852.

History of the Edmondson Family. c. 1852.

A Key to Uncle Tom's Cabin: *Presenting the Original Facts and
Documents upon Which the Story Is Founded.* 1853, 1854.

*Uncle Sam's Emancipation; Earthly Care, a Heavenly Discipline;
and Other Sketches.* 1853.

The Coral King. 1853.

Letter to the Ladies' New Anti-Slavery Society of Glasgow.
c. 1853.

Sunny Memories of Foreign Lands. 1854. 2 vols.

Notice of the Boston Anti-Slavery Bazaar. c. 1854.

First Geography for Children. 1855.

The May Flower and Miscellaneous Writings. 1855.

The Christian Slave. 1855.

What Should We Do without the Bible? c. 1855.

Dred: A Tale of the Great Dismal Swamp. 1856. 2 vols.

Mrs. H. B. Stowe on Dr. Monod and the American Tract Society; Considered in Relation to American Slavery. 1858.

My Expectation. 1858.

My Strength. 1858.

Things That Cannot Be Shaken. 1858.

Strong Consolation; or, God a Refuge and Strength. 1858.

A Word to the Sorrowful. 1858.

Our Charley, and What to Do with Him. 1858.

Harriet Beecher Stowe on the American Board of Commissioners for Foreign Missions. c. 1858.

The Minister's Wooing. 1859.

The Pearl of Orr's Island: A Story of the Coast of Maine. 1862.

Agnes of Sorrento. 1862.

A Reply to The Affectionate and Christian Address of Many Thousands of Women of Great Britain and Ireland, to Their Sisters, the Women of the United States: *In Behalf of Many Thousands of American Women.* 1863.

Primitive Christian Experience. c. 1863.

The Ravages of a Carpet. c. 1864.

House and Home Papers. 1865.

Stories about Our Dogs. 1865.

Little Foxes. 1866.

Religious Poems. 1867.

The Daisy's First Winter and Other Stories. 1867.

Queer Little People. 1867.

The Chimney-Corner. 1868.

Men of Our Times; or, Leading Patriots of the Day. 1868.

Oldtown Folks. 1869.

The American Woman's Home; or, Principles of Domestic Science (with Catherine E. Beecher). 1869, 1870 (as *Principles of Domestic Science*), 1874 (as *The New Housekeeper's Manual*).

Lady Byron Vindicated: A History of the Byron Controversy from Its Beginning in 1816 to the Present Time. 1870.

Little Pussy Willow. 1870.

Pink and White Tyranny: A Society Novel. 1871.

My Wife and I; or, Harry Henderson's History. 1871.

Have You Seen It? Letter from Mrs. Stowe to Miss Kate Reignolds. c. 1871.

Sam Lawson's Oldtown Fireside Stories. 1872.

"He's Coming To-morrow." c. 1872.

Palmetto-Leaves. 1873.

Woman in Sacred History. 1873.

We and Our Neighbors; or, The Records of an Unfashionable Street. 1875.

Betty Bright Idea. 1876.

Footsteps of the Master. 1877.

Poganuc People: Their Loves and Lives. 1878.

A Dog's Mission; or, The Story of the Old Avery House, and Other Stories. 1881.

Flowers and Fruit from the Writings of Harriet Beecher Stowe. Ed. Abbie H. Fairfield. 1888.

Dialogues and Scenes from the Writings of Harriet Beecher Stowe. Ed. Emily Weaver. 1889.

Life of Harriet Beecher Stowe Compiled from Her Letters and Journals. Ed. Charles Edward Stowe. 1889.

Writings. 1896. 16 vols.

Life and Letters. Ed. Annie Fields. 1897.

Collected Poems. Ed. John Michael Moran, Jr. 1967.

Regional Sketches: New England and Florida. Ed. John R. Adams. 1972.

Uncle Tom's Cabin; The Minister's Wooing; Oldtown Folks. 1982.

Works about
Harriet Beecher Stowe and
Uncle Tom's Cabin

Anderson, Beatrice A. "Uncle Tom: A Hero at Last." *American Transcendental Quarterly* 5 (1991): 95–108.

Askeland, Lori. "Remodeling the Model Home in *Uncle Tom's Cabin* and *Beloved.*" *American Literature* 64 (1992): 785–805.

Baldwin, James. "Everybody's Protest Novel." *Partisan Review* 16 (1949): 578–85.

Banks, Marva. "*Uncle Tom's Cabin* and Antebellum Black Response." In *Readers in History: Nineteenth-Century American Literature and the Contexts of Response,* ed. James L. Machor. Baltimore: Johns Hopkins University Press, 1993, pp. 209–27.

Bellin, Joshua D. "Up to Heaven's Gate, Down in Earth's Dust: The Politics of Judgment in *Uncle Tom's Cabin.*" *American Literature* 65 (1993): 275–95.

Brown, Gillian. "Getting in the Kitchen with Dinah: Domestic Politics in *Uncle Tom's Cabin.*" *American Quarterly* 36 (1984): 503–23.

Camfield, Gregg. "The Moral Aesthetics of Sentimentality: A Missing Key to *Uncle Tom's Cabin.*" *Nineteenth-Century Literature* 43 (1988–89): 319–45.

DeCanio, Stephen J. "*Uncle Tom's Cabin:* A Reappraisal." *Centennial Review* 34 (1990): 587–93.

Fiedler, Leslie. "Home as Heaven, Home as Hell: Uncle Tom's Canon." In *Rewriting the Dream: Reflections on the Changing American Canon,* ed. W. M. Verhoeven. Amsterdam: Rodopi, 1992, pp. 22–42.

Fluck, Winfried. "The Power and Failure of Representation in Harriet Beecher Stowe's *Uncle Tom's Cabin.*" *New Literary History* 23 (1992): 319–38.

Grinstein, Alexander. "*Uncle Tom's Cabin* and Harriet Beecher Stowe: Beating Fantasies and Thoughts of Death." *American Imago* 40 (1983): 115–44.

Hedrick, Joan B. *Harriet Beecher Stowe: A Life.* New York: Oxford University Press, 1994.

Hirsch, Stephen A. "Uncle Tomitudes: The Popular Reaction to *Uncle Tom's Cabin.*" *Studies in the American Renaissance,* 1978, pp. 303–30.

Hovet, Theodore R. "Modernization and the American Fall into Slavery in *Uncle Tom's Cabin.*" *New England Quarterly* 54 (1981): 499–518.

Jehlen, Myra. "The Family Militant: Domesticity versus Slavery in *Uncle Tom's Cabin.*" *Criticism* 31 (1989): 383–400.

Joswick, Thomas P. " 'The Crown without the Conflict': Religious Values and Moral Reasoning in *Uncle Tom's Cabin.*" *Nineteenth-Century Literature* 39 (1984–85): 253–74.

Kimball, Gayle. *The Religious Ideas of Harriet Beecher Stowe: Her Gospel of Womanhood.* New York: Mellen Press, 1982.

Kirkham, E. Bruce. *The Building of* Uncle Tom's Cabin. Knoxville: University of Tennessee Press, 1977.

Krog, Carl E. "Women, Slaves, and Family in *Uncle Tom's Cabin:* Symbolic Battleground in Antebellum America." *Midwest Quarterly* 31 (1990): 252–69.

Lant, Kathleen Margaret. "The Unsung Hero of *Uncle Tom's Cabin.*" *American Studies* 28 (1987): 47–71.

Lowance, Mason I., Jr.; Wesbrook, Ellen E.; and De Prospo, R. C., ed. *The Stowe Debate: Rhetorical Strategies in* Uncle Tom's Cabin. Amherst: University of Massachusetts Press, 1994.

McConnell, Frank D. "Uncle Tom and the Avant-Garde." *Massachusetts Review* 16 (1975): 732–45.

Moers, Ellen. *Harriet Beecher Stowe and American Literature.* Hartford, CT: Stowe-Day Foundation, 1978.

Prior, Moody E. "Mrs. Stowe's Uncle Tom." *Critical Inquiry* 5 (1978–79): 635–50.

Railton, Stephen. "Mothers, Husbands, and Uncle Tom."
Georgia Review 38 (1984): 129–44.

Reynolds, Moira Davison. Uncle Tom's Cabin *and Mid-Nineteenth Century United States: Pen and Conscience.*
Jefferson, NC: McFarland, 1985.

Romero, Lora. "Bio-Political Resistance in Domestic Ideology
and *Uncle Tom's Cabin." American Literary History* 1 (1989):
715–34.

Sarson, Steven. "Harriet Beecher Stowe and American Slavery."
New Comparison 7 (Summer 1989): 33–45.

Short, Bryan C. "Stowe, Dickinson, and the Rhetoric of
Modernism." *Arizona Quarterly* 47 (1991): 1–16.

Smylie, James H. "*Uncle Tom's Cabin* Revisited: The Bible, the
Romantic Imagination, and the Sympathies of Christ."
Interpretation 27 (1973): 67–85.

Sundquist, Eric J., ed. *New Essays on* Uncle Tom's Cabin.
Cambridge: Cambridge University Press, 1986.

Wagenknecht, Edward. *Harriet Beecher Stowe: The Known and
the Unknown.* New York: Oxford University Press, 1965.

Wardley, Lynn. "Relic, Fetish, Femmage: The Aesthetics of
Sentiment in the Work of Stowe." *Yale Journal of Criticism* 5
(1992): 165–91.

Warhol, Robyn R. "Politics and Persuasion: *Uncle Tom's Cabin*
as a Realist Novel." *Essays in Literature* 13 (1986): 283–98.

White, Isabelle. "The Uses of Death in *Uncle Tom's Cabin."
American Studies* 26 (1985): 5–17.

Whitney, Lisa. "In the Shadow of *Uncle Tom's Cabin:* Stowe's
Vision of Slavery from the Great Dismal Swamp." *New
England Quarterly* 66 (1993): 552–69.

Yellin, Jean Fagan. "Harriet Beecher Stowe." In Yellin's *The
Intricate Knot: Black Figures in American Literature.* New
York: New York University Press, 1972, pp. 121–53.

Zwarg, Christina. "Fathering the Blackface in *Uncle Tom's
Cabin." Novel* 22 (1989): 274–87.

Index of
Themes and Ideas

LEGREE, SIMON: as Antichrist, 56; Augustine St. Clare contrasted with, 34–35; haunted garret of, 20–21; mother of,
20; and his role in the novel, 5–6, 18–21, 36; Tom sold to,
18, 24

LIBERIA, and its role in the novel, 21–22, 45

LITTLE WOMEN (Alcott), and how it compares, 38

LOKER, TOM, and his role in the novel, 12, 15, 34

MAMMY, and her role in the novel, 15

MARKS, and his role in the novel, 12, 15, 34, 40

MOTHERHOOD, as theme, 12, 16, 21, 47–49, 57–59

PIONEERS, THE (Cooper), and how it compares, 40

PRUE, and her role in the novel, 16

ST. CLARE, ALFRED, and his role in the novel, 16–17, 41

ST. CLARE, AUGUSTINE: death of, 18; and Eva's death, 17–18;
and evil, 56; Legree contrasted with, 34–35; and his role in
the novel, 15–18, 20, 23

ST. CLARE, EVANGELINE ("Little Eva"): death of, 17, 23, 37;
and her role in the novel, 14–18, 23, 44; Tom's relationship
with, 16–18, 19, 20; and Topsy, 16–18, 24

ST. CLARE, HENRIQUE, and his role in the novel, 16–17, 41

ST. CLARE, MARIE, and her role in the novel, 15–18, 24, 41

ST. CLARE, OPHELIA, and her role in the novel, 15–18, 21,
24, 41

SCARLET LETTER, THE (Hawthorne), and how it compares, 6

SHELBY, GEORGE, and his role in the novel, 11, 13, 21

SHELBY, MR., and his role in the novel, 10–13, 16, 18, 21,
42, 45